ITALIANS FORWARD

ITALIANS FORWARD

A Visual History of the Italian
Community in Great Britain

TERRI COLPI

MAINSTREAM
PUBLISHING

EDINBURGH AND LONDON

First published in Great Britain 1991 by
MAINSTREAM PUBLISHING COMPANY (EDINBURGH) LTD
7 Albany, Street
Edinburgh EH1 3UG

ISBN 1 85158 349 1

A catalogue record for this book is available from the British Library.
Phototypeset in 10/12pt Palatino by Intype, London
Printed in Great Britain by the Bath Press, Bath

The publisher gratefully acknowledges the financial assistance from the Scottish Arts Council in the production of this volume.

Jacket Illustrations:

FRONT COVER
Main Picture Two hundred Signorine arrive at Victoria Station,
London, 1950 *(Credit: Topham Picture Source)*
Insert A. Canale with his Ice-cream Barrow at Cwmpare, Rhonnda,
1924 *(Credit: C. Batstone)*

BACK COVER
Italy wins the World Cup, Bedford, 1982
(Credit: Bedfordshire Times)

In memory of my grandfather
Dolfè di Stagnedo

Contents

Acknowledgments

Without the active collaboration of Italians resident in Great Britain from the first to the fifth generation, from all walks of life, from the north of Scotland to the south of England and Wales, this book would not have been possible. Indeed, they and many thousands like them are not only the subject of the book, they are the inspiration for it.

My greatest single debt is to the British Italian fortnightly newspaper *La Voce degli Italiani in Gran Bretagna* and specifically *Padre* Gaetano Parolin for allowing me unlimited access to their photographic archives. Their material relating particularly to the 1960s and 1970s strengthened considerably my coverage of those periods.

I must give my most sincere and heartfelt thanks to all those people who so generously and trustingly lent me photographs and documents: without their cooperation, this book would not have been possible. No one was kinder than Anthony Rea of Manchester whose personal collection of old photographs of the Ancoats Italian Colony is second to none. He very generously allowed me to use several of his prize examples. Ultimately, from a large collection, a selection of around 250 photographs had painstakingly to be made.

I would also like to thank all the people listed below, with whom I spoke during the research for the book: without those dialogues, the book would have been deprived of vast seams of fascinating information and vital factual corroboration, and I would have been deprived of many absorbing conversations and many new friends and acquaintances. I hope all of them, and all those who read *Italians Forward* feel that I have at least come some way towards doing justice to my theme. Any errors remain of course my sole responsibility, including any errors of omission from the following list.

Rita Aceto, Bedford; Anna Alonzi, Edinburgh; Roland Antonelli, Manchester; Aldo Bacchetta, Porth; Bruno Bartolomei, Barga; Rodolfo Benacci, Greenock; *Padre* Silvano Bertapelle, Woking; *Cav.* Rando Bertoia, Glasgow; *Cav.* Bruno Besagni, Olive Besagni, London; *Cav.* Luigi Beschizza, Essex; *Cav.* Pietro Beschizza, Middlesex; Edwin Bicocchi, Aberdeen; Tommaso Bruccoleri, London; Wolfgang Bucci, London; Pino Buglione, Derby; *Console Generale* Rodolfo Buonavita, Edinburgh; *Cav.* Enrico Casci, Falkirk; Lorenzo Castello, London; Monty Cattini, London; Alberto Cavalli, London; Luigi Cavandoli, Manchester; Bruno Cervi, London; *Cav.* Romolo Chiocconi, Glasgow; *Cav.* Amilcare Cima, Padivarma; Louis Coletti, Pina Coletti, Edinburgh; Armo Collini, London; Rodolfo Colpi, Martin Colpi, Milngavie; Antonio Conetta, Glasgow; Bishop Mario Conti, Aberdeen; Victor Crolla, Edinburgh; Guido Cruci, Essex; *Cav.* Nicola Cua, Wallington; Domenica De Marco Cullen, Edinburgh; *Console Generale* Gabriele De Ceglie, London; *Cav.* Richard De Marco, Edinburgh; *Padre* Carmelo Di Giovanni, London; Ann Marie Di Mambro, Hamilton; Bert Di Mambro, Merthyr Tydfil; Renza Donati, Dingwall; the late *Cav.* Guiseppe Dorà and his family, Beith; Carlo Edoni, Glasgow; Lillie Ferrari, London; Kathleen Fusco, Edinburgh; *Comm.* Giuseppe Giacon, London; Angelo Giovanazzi, Glasgow; *Cav.* Fulvio Giretti, Nottingham; Gabriele Grandi, London; Louis Granelli, Manchester; *Cav.* Gino Guarnieri, London; *Cav.* Fortunato Iannetta, St Andrews; *Cav.* Riccardo Lombardelli, Leicester; *Comm.* Benedetto Longinotti, London; Damiana Maestri, Manchester; Pino Maestri, London; Arturo Malvermi, London; the Mancini family, Ayr; Antonio Manfredi, Leigh; Peter Marchetti, Olga Marchetti, Glasgow; *Console* Sergio Mercuri, Manchester; Dr Eileen Millar, Glasgow; *Comm.Avv.* Tino Moscardini, Glasgow; John Muir, Orkney; *Cav.* Roberta Mutti, London; Dr Remo Nanetti, Glasgow; Raimondo Nante, London; *Vice Console* Fabrizio Necchi, Aberdeen; Joan Ottolini, Glasgow; the late *Cav.* Alessandro and Charles Pacitti, Glasgow; Gina Pacitti, Glasgow; Claudia Petretti, Edinburgh; *Cav.* Elio Poli, Tarbolton; Alice Arcari Pollard, Edinburgh; Silvia Quarantelli, Aberdeen; Olga Raffaeta, Pietrasanta; Maria Renucci, Glasgow; Florindo Rizzi, London; Elpidio Rossi, Chiavari; Monsignor Gaetano Rossi, Glasgow; Elena Salvoni, London; Amadeo Sarti, Glasgow; *Cav.* Maria Schiavo, Cardiff; *Cav.* Giorgio Scola, Reading; *Comm.* Renzo Serafini, Inverness; Rita Sidoli,

Swansea; Dr Lucio Sponza, London; Paolo Trainotti, London; Ronaldo Zanrè, London; Antony Zanrè, Norina Zanrè, Aberdeen; Adolfo Zaccardelli, Edinburgh, *Padre* Pietro Zorza, Glasgow.

On the technical side I am grateful to Tony Lee at Oxford University for reproducing many old photographs for me.

Lastly, I would like to thank my assistant, Michela Galelli, for her practical help and unfailing enthusiasm throughout the compilation of *Italians Forward*.

Introduction

The aim of *Italians Forward* is to present a complete visual history of the Italian Community in Great Britain from the middle of the nineteenth century to the present day. As a visual history, rather than just a book of pictures, the captions to the photographs are as important as the images themselves. Although every picture does indeed tell a story, to understand more of the whole story, some words can undoubtedly be helpful. These captions therefore take the photographs as a starting point and through the pages of *Italians Forward*, the tale unfolds.

Inevitably, as the camera came into use only as the nineteenth century advanced, greater reliance on words is necessary in outlining the main aspects of those early years and in describing the pioneering migrants of long ago. However, where possible, photographs and drawings have been included, although allowance must be made for the poorer condition today of those early photographic images. Towards the end of the 1800s and the early 1900s, the greater availability of photographs allows the story to take the form maintained for the rest of the book.

A chapter has been devoted to each of the ten decades of the twentieth century (except for the golden era of the 1920s and 1930s which are treated together). A brief introduction highlights key aspects of Italian Community development and activity during that decade, and then the photographs take over. Priority is given to occupations; the overwhelming reason for Italians coming to Britain was not the weather! They came here to work. They worked for themselves, they worked for their relations and families, they worked for more prominent individuals from their village of origin in Italy, or more recently, they seized opportunities to work for British industry and companies in need of reliable, hardworking men and women. They came to work to earn money to support their families, sometimes with them in Britain, sometimes not. It is families and family life that form the second set of photographs within each chapter.

Photographs have always been important to migrants and their families at home in Italy. When people are separated by great distances for long periods of time, it becomes important to try and keep in touch as best they can, and sending photographs plays a role. There are many fine photographic family portraits from fifty to ninety years ago showing dignified, well dressed groups, often in formal, photographic studio settings. Italians always like to cut a *bella figura* and there are many excellent examples here. The family story behind the image is brought out in the captions, often forming a potted, yet fascinating family history. From these, it becomes clear that migration is rarely a one-off static process. Rather a migrant establishes a connection with a new environment, from which travel to Italy and back again to the new country takes place for the pioneering migrant, and then his family, relations and friends.

The third feature in each chapter is recreational activity and Community life. The institutions of the Italian Community and the highlights of the year — such as processions, outings and entertainment — are shown. Some events, such as the procession of the *Madonna del Carmine* in London, an annual event since 1883, can be seen at several times in their 'lives'! The impact of Mussolini and the Italian fascist period of the 1920s and 1930s on the Community before and during the Second World War are also covered. Remember, Italy and Britain fought on the same side in the First World War, but not in the Second.

Finally, in terms of organisation and coverage of the book, I have tried to present a balanced geographic coverage of the Italian presence in this country. Photographs reach as far north as Inverness in Scotland, and as far south as Paignton in Devon. Within this, the major Italian Communities of London, Bedford and Peterborough, Manchester, Glasgow and Edinburgh are all represented.

Italians Forward is for two sets of readers. Firstly, of course, it is a book for members of the Community themselves. For a Community entering, in some areas, a fifth or sixth generation, it can be hard to pass on by word of mouth the memories of the early years. So many of the former occupations and ways of life of the early Italian immigrants are no longer visible and words alone cannot conjure up these images for us. But this book has also been produced to help make people of Italian heritage in one area of the country more aware of other towns and cities with an Italian presence. The whole picture is rich and varied, a 'gorgeous mosaic' which is all too rarely seen or appreciated in its totality.

Italians Forward is also written for people outside the Community, like my own husband, who knew little of the Italians in Britain until he met me. As the Italian Community has grown, through hard work and not a little suffering, it has undoubtedly prospered. Almost all the Italian migrants have been entrepreneurs. Indeed, many arrived exhibiting new skills and talents, or bringing new products and services to supply to the local people; the wide range of, often specialist, crafts and services they provided over the generations is shown here. Clues are also given about the reasons for their remarkable success in all aspects of the food and catering business. To those not directly in the Italian Community, this book shows the range of Italian contribution to Britain both yesterday and today.

It is particularly important now, as the Italians have achieved prosperity, social acceptance and increasing local and national prominence, to tell their story. Today, of course, the interest of the British people in their Italian Community strengthens as they themselves try to cope with Britain's occasionally reluctant, but seemingly irreversible, greater involvement in the wider European community. When you are already Italian, as well as British, or British as well as Italian, you are better equipped for 1992 and beyond than most of your fellow citizens. Italians Forward!

ITALIANS FORWARD

CHAPTER ONE

The Nineteenth Century

There had been Italian scholars, musicians and artists present in Great Britain throughout the Middle Ages. Just before the starting point of our visual history, another important group of men began to arrive at around the turn of the nineteenth century. These were skilled craftsmen from northern Italy who settled and set up businesses, mostly in London and Manchester, in the areas of Clerkenwell and Ancoats respectively. It was around the nuclei formed by the craftsmen that a second, poorer wave of immigrants began to congregate. It is here that our visual history begins.

The influx of poor Italian immigrants began in the 1820s and 1830s, and built up gradually throughout the middle of the nineteenth century. They came from the Tuscan and Emilian Appenines, from tiny isolated hamlets and from the countryside just north of Naples — the *Ciociaria*. Virtually all of these people walked to this country, crossing the channel by ferry. They were part of a much larger exodus from Italy of people in search of work at that time.

It was these migrants who were responsible for the formation of 'Little Italy' in Clerkenwell. The Colony was founded on street musicianship, with organ grinding the most popular occupation of the mid-nineteenth century. From London, there was a gradual dispersal and movement northwards and the Manchester Italian Colony of Ancoats was established not long after the Clerkenwell Community.

One of the key figures in the organisation both of emigration from Italy and the control of the migrants when they reached this country, in terms of work, food and lodgings, was the *padrone*. A contract would be issued to a boy before leaving Italy under which he was bound to a *padrone*, usually for a period of two to three years. Conditions were often harsh, but many boys completed their contracts and were then free to work for themselves, spending their earnings on their own organ or taking up other employment.

In addition to organ grinding and street entertainment, there were other occupational groups within the early Colony. These included the *figurinai*, or makers and sellers of small statuettes. These travelling semi-skilled craftsmen began to arrive in London in the 1850s and then spread out across the rest of the country, reaching Scotland by the 1870s. Then there were the *arrotini*, knife grinders, who arrived in the 1870s, and also of note were the highly skilled mosaic and *terrazzo* craftsmen who arrived from the 1880s and were often called to specific locations for important works.

By the 1880s, there was a decline in organ grinding. With this decline, a natural move into itinerant street selling of food occurred. Initially, roasted chestnuts were sold in winter and the *padrone* controlled and organised the import of chestnuts from the mountain valleys of Italy. However, very soon the street selling of ice-cream developed as an occupation. Initially, the milk was boiled in domestic kitchens in Clerkenwell and Ancoats and frozen out of doors in the morning. The ice-cream was then wheeled around the streets to better residential areas. This was to prove a very lucrative field of activity for the Italians and one which between 1880 and 1900 caused the British Italian Community quite literally to triple in numbers.

The Colony in London was, by the 1880s, very well organised internally with the establishment of several institutions. An Italian school, the *Mazzini Garibaldi Club*, the Italian Church of St Peter's and the Italian Hospital were all in place by the turn of the century. It was in the 1880s and 1890s that the first Italians settled permanently in Wales and Scotland; here too the foundations for ice-cream businesses and the small café were laid.

STREET MUSICIANS, LONDON, 1818

The first itinerant street musicians from Italy began to arrive in London long before the unification of Italy in 1861. The female vocalist and violinist duetting in this lively street-scene most probably came from the Savoy mountain region between France and Italy and are typical of European street entertainment of the eighteenth century. The man in the middle, however, 'grinding' his hand held organ, would have come from the Duchy of Parma and he heralds the new era of immigration and of mechanical street instruments which required no skill to play. By the 1830s organs of various types had replaced the traditional instruments and so numerous were the Italian organ grinders that by the late Victorian era these were increasingly considered a street nuisance. (*Credit: British Museum*)

AN ITALIAN STREET MUSICIAN WITH MONKEYS OUTSIDE THE ORIGINAL CADBURY SHOP, BIRMINGHAM, C. 1830

Surrounded by passers by, the musician plays on his *zampogne*. This is a wind instrument, similar to the Scottish bagpipes, and indeed we can see the bag tucked under his left arm as he picks out the notes on the pipe. The *zampogne* are traditional to the *Ciociaria* area of Italy between Rome and Naples, and thus tell us precisely the origin of the musician. He is also accompanied by no less than five monkeys which added to the general entertainment. The monkeys were trained to pick up coins thrown by passers by and the most intelligent could distinguish between coins and other round metal objects. On his back the musician also has a small organ which he played by simply grinding the handle and which presumably offered relief from puffing away on the *zampogne*. (*Credit: Cadbury Ltd*)

THE ORGAN GRINDERS QUARTERS, HATTON GARDEN, LONDON, 1875

During the nineteenth century the Italian Colony of London was centred around Hatton Garden and Leather Lane. The majority of the immigrants came from hamlets in the Tuscan and Emilian Appenines and from the mountain villages in the Liri Valleys of the *Ciociaria*. Most had walked to London. By the 1840s they had established 'Little Italy' based on organ grinding and other forms of street entertainment. In the drawing we see a barrel or piano organ being pulled along and also several people carrying the smaller hand-held organs on their backs. Both were 'played' by grinding a handle. From the Colony the organ grinders and other itinerant street musicians set out to play their music around London. Many people did not own an organ, but hired one on a daily basis from a *padrone* who controlled large numbers of the street musicians in this way. From 1865, most of the organs were made by either Chiappa or Antonelli Spinelli & Rossi. (*Credit: The Graphic*)

ANTONIO AND PAOLINA REA WITH THEIR BARREL ORGAN, CHESTER, 1897
The couple emigrated from Arpino (Fr) in 1895, spent some time in London and then moved northward, in the search for new territories, to Chester. Their organ was most probably made by either Robino or Antonelli of Manchester. After his partnership with Spinelli & Rossi in Clerkenwell, Domenico Antonelli left London for Manchester where, in 1894, he set up his own firm on the corner of Great Ancoats Street and Blossom Street in the Italian Colony, and went on to become the main barrel organ supplier for the north of England. Robino worked for Antonelli and then set up a small firm of his own, being famous for his original tunes.
(*Credit: A. Rea*)

A *FIGURINAIO*, LONDON, 1883

The boy in this cartoon, selling his statuettes on a specially designed portable display shelf, would have been part of a group of *figurinai*, itinerant makers and sellers of statuettes, who came from the province of Lucca in Tuscany. Such groups began to arrive in London from the late 1850s. They travelled and worked as a team of between five and seven men, including one or two boys, all under the control of a *padrone*. They carried all their tools, moulds and paints in large wooden chests as they travelled and each had his own job in the production and selling of the statuettes. Glasgow represented the northern-most market in a British trip and this probably explains why so many eventually settled there and in nearby Paisley.
(*Credit: Punch*)

THE ITALIAN BOY, LONDON, 1856

Apparently, it had taken Pietro, here shown exhibiting his little box which contained two white mice, a whole year to grind and pipe his way from Italy to the shores of the Channel. He crossed in April 1856 from Boulogne and came to London where his trade of street entertaining was little better than begging. His little organ had been confiscated by his *padrone* and given to another boy. The white mice were to be his credentials for appealing to the charity of passers by. The scandal of young boys, often kept in poor conditions, made to work under a 'contract' with a *padrone* caused concern in Victorian society, but this was the era of child factory workers and boy chimney-sweeps.
(*Credit: Leisure Hour*)

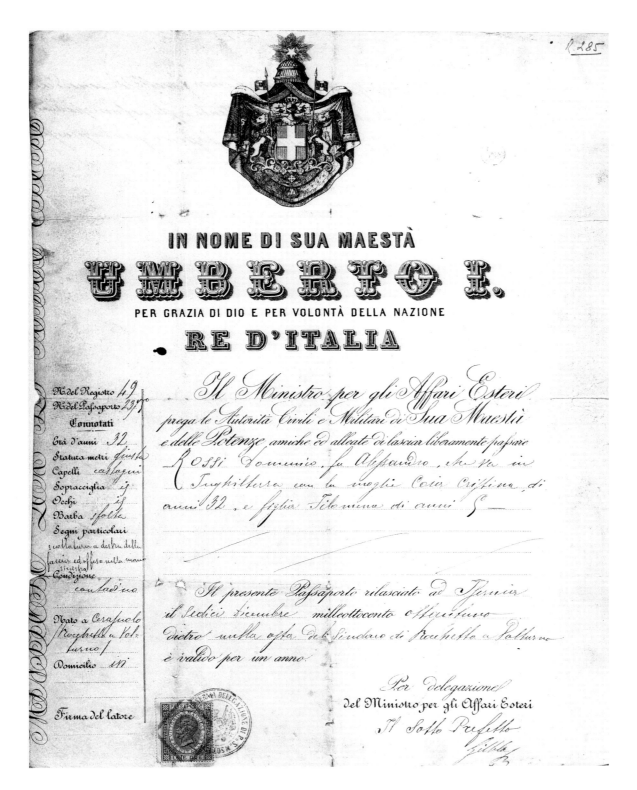

AN ITALIAN PASSPORT, 1881

In the name of Umberto I of Italy, this passport — a single sheet — asks that Domenico Rossi, his wife Cristina Coia and their daughter Filomena aged nine, be given free passage on their journey to England. Issued at Isernia on 16 December 1881, with a validity of one year, their origin was the hamlet of Cerasuolo, in the *comune* of Rocchetta al Volturno (Is). In the absence of a photograph we can only imagine how Domenico Rossi looked with his medium height, dark hair, thick beard, burn-mark on the right-hand side of his face and injured left hand! No indication is given of his proposed destination or occupation in England, and although he had been a land peasant (*Condizione Contadino*) he did manage to pay the two lire stamp for the passport.
(*Credit: Console S. Mercuri*)

AN ICE-CREAM MAKER, CAROLINE PLACE, CLERKENWELL, LONDON, C. 1890
Caroline Place was a cul-de-sac off Bakers Row measuring 18 feet long and just 3 to 4 feet wide. It contained four houses with 22 occupants, almost exclusively Italian. Indoors the milk mixture for ice-cream was boiled in the evening and left to cool overnight. In the morning, outside in such courtyards, by using a cylindrical zinc drum, inside a wooden barrel, the ice-cream was made. The space between the two was packed with ice and salt. (The salt caused the ice to melt to the required temperature, forming a brine.) The milk mixture was then poured into the inner cylinder and by hand-turning it, the milk eventually froze and the ice-cream formed. The wheel barrow on the left would then be used to push the ice-cream around the streets. Just behind the barrow we can see the zinc drums, with lids, which were used to transport the ice-cream. At the turn of the century there were around 900 such ice-cream barrows in Clerkenwell.
(Credit: Finsbury Library)

ICE-CREAM VENDOR, LONDON, C. 1890
Ice-cream carts and barrows came in various varieties and forms, all hand-made and decorated by the ice-cream men themselves. This one is a good example of the *Baldacchino*, or canopied sort. In these early days, there were no cones or wafers and the ice-cream was served in little 'licking glasses', visible, turned upside down, on the right-hand side of the barrow counter. These were rinsed out between customers, a practice which increasingly caused hygiene concern. The ice-cream industry was later saved by the introduction of the cone and wafer biscuit.
(*Credit: R. Pomeroy*)

THE ITALIAN EXHIBITION, EARLS COURT, LONDON, 1888
Organised by the newly formed Italian Chamber of Commerce, this exhibition gave all sorts of Italian businesses in operation in Britain their first opportunity to promote themselves in an organised manner. This particular display, which featured 'Neopolitan Iced Drinks', pictures Olivia Coppola behind the stall and was most probably amongst the ice-cream trade's first exhibits in this country. (*Credit: A. Pompa*)

ITALIAN SUNDAY SCHOOL, LONDON, 1875

On Sunday and in the evenings priests of the Italian Church, St Peter's, imparted the three Rs to Italian men, women and children alike. The vast majority of the poor Italian immigrants of this era were illiterate, having come from tiny isolated mountain villages. Giuseppe Mazzini, the Italian patriot who had been a political exile in London in the 1840s, had established a school to help educate the people of the Colony. After the founding of St Peter's in 1864, however, the main social initiatives were taken by the Italian priests. Naturally when the school expanded into a day school, there was much opposition to their efforts from the *padroni* of the Colony since boys were taken away from their work to attend classes. (*Credit: The Graphic*)

THE INTERIOR, ST PETER'S ITALIAN CHURCH, CLERKENWELL, LONDON

When in 1844, San Vincenzo Pallotti sent one of his missionary priests to help the Italian Colony of London, he hoped eventually to establish a church for them. This dream was realised in 1864 when St Peter's was inaugurated. Built in Hatton Wall, in the heart of the Italian Colony, the church and the other institutions established by the priests, such as the school, became the heart as well as the soul of the Italian Community. Designed in the Italianate style, based on a scaled down version of the Basilica San Crisogono in Rome, this beautiful church initially had its entrance on Little Saffron Hill. After much housing clearance and demolition, Clerkenwell Road was opened in 1878 and the entrance to the church as it is today was opened. The organ was installed in 1887 when the church choir was established. (*Credit: T. Colpi*)

WASHER WOMEN CHAT, THE CLERKENWELL ITALIAN COLONY, LONDON, C. 1890
A common occupation for women was laundry work. They would collect laundry and carry it in oval zinc baths to the public wash-houses where they paid to wash and dry it, initially over fires and later over gas boilers. They then carried the laundry home to iron it, using solid 'irons' of different sizes. At the turn of the century, when the catering-based Soho Italian Community was expanding, many of the women in the poorer Clerkenwell quarter would take in laundry from the waiters and their families. Each woman worked for specific families, collecting laundry on a weekly basis. This occupation was still common in the 1920s and 1930s. (*Credit: Armfelt*)

PLAYING *MORRA*, THE ITALIAN COLONY, LONDON, C. 1890
A popular Italian guessing game in which two players extend their right hand, closed in a fist, and as they open one or more fingers, a third player tries to guess the total number of extended fingers. *Morra* players and spectators can become extremely excited in the confusion of the game — it was often banned from the Italian club houses due to the heated disputes which could break out. (*Credit: Armfelt*)

CHAPTER TWO

The 1900s

During the 1900s, the Italians continued to spread out, travelling north and west from London. Whereas in the last century, the immigrants had congregated in the large urban centres, now many smaller towns saw their first Italian families arriving and settling, for example in Fraserburgh in Aberdeenshire and Treorchy in Rhondda. These settlers were true pioneers, boldly going where no Italian had been before, finding new territories, markets and pitches. Many had been itinerant street-sellers of food in the cities and had done well enough to be able to acquire their own permanent premises. All this activity generated a continuing requirement, of course, for extra hands from Italy.

There was no shortage of young people in Italy anxious to migrate and seek their fortune abroad in the early years of the twentieth century. Due to the 1905 Aliens Act, it was necessary for the prospective migrant to have an arrangement for work and accommodation with someone already established in Britain. 'Chains' developed whereby family networks in Britain 'called for' extra help and *padroni* 'brought over' large numbers of mainly young male and female offspring, brothers, sisters, cousins, nephews, nieces and *paesani*. Gradually entire families were transferred from Italy and particular towns in this country began to build up connections with specific source villages in Italy. This was how 'chain' migration operated and the result was that many towns gained their own distinctive little Italian Communities.

The migrants from Bardi (Pr) went to London and the Welsh valleys; those from Borgo Val di Taro (Pr) remained mainly in London, but some ventured as far north as Aberdeen; those from Barga (Lu) mainly settled in Glasgow and Paisley; and those from Picinisco and other villages in the province of Frosinone, spread across the whole country.

At this time, life in the two main Colonies of Clerkenwell and Ancoats really was like 'Little Italy'. All sorts of goods and services were provided for Italians by other Italians, giving the Community a high degree of self-sufficiency. Migrants had nothing to fear as they arrived into the bosom of the Colony, sponsored as they were by family and friends. Specialist Italian 'Provisions Shops' began to open, supplying their local Italian Colonies with food from home. The Italian way of life was celebrated by the Italian Church with the annual processions of the *Madonna* through the streets.

It was at this time, also, that the second Italian Colony of London, in Soho, was beginning to take root, based on the growth of the catering industry — hotels, clubs, and later restaurants in the West End of London. This was separate and distinct from the Clerkenwell Colony and had its own growing sense of community.

Elsewhere in the country, however, there was not much organised activity or feeling of 'community' due to long working hours in many occupations and the sheer geographical distance between the Italians. However, some Italian Community newspapers did exist at this time, and they helped people to keep in touch with community news and issues.

ICE-CREAM SELLERS, WREXHAM, C. 1905
Standing in the cart is Pietro Guazelli who emigrated to Britain in 1880 from the *Garfagnana* in Tuscany. The two *garzoni*, or boys, worked for him selling ice-cream in summer, and in the winter they brought consignments of chestnuts from Italy which they roasted and sold around the streets in a similar manner. Just visible on the side of the cart are the words 'Hokey Pokey', reputed to have derived from the local version of the Italian *'ecco un poco'*, meaning 'here is a little', said when dispensing the ice-cream into the licking glasses. The ice-cream men became known as the 'Hokey Pokey Men'. (*Credit: P. Cresci*)

A RENUCCI BAKERY HORSE AND CART MAKING DELIVERIES, GLASGOW, EARLY 1900s
See top photo on p. 30. (*Credit: M. Renucci*)

TERRONI AND SONS, CLERKENWELL ROAD, LONDON, C. 1900
Luigi Terroni left Pontremoli (Ms) in 1870, made his way to Paris on foot and, a few years later, to London. In 1890 he opened his provisions shop next door to the Italian Church. The business remained in Terroni family ownership until the 1980s when it was bought by Domenico Annessa from the Bedford Italian Community. It continues to benefit from its proximity to the church and Sunday is its busiest day as Italians return to 'Little Italy' from all areas of London for Mass at St Peter's and groceries at Terroni. (*Credit: Finsbury Library*)

THE PARMIGIANI COMESTIBILI PROVISIONS SHOP, LONDON, C. 1900
At the corner of Warner Street and Great Bath Street (now Topham Street), this store was at the northern end of the old Italian Colony. Outside we see a parked ice-cream barrow and next door, on the right, an Italian barber's shop. These shops not only provided the Italian Community with their household needs and in the case of the barber's, hair cuts and shaves, but they also acted as meeting places where information and gossip could be exchanged. This was particularly true of the barber's shop where men could gather in an almost club-like atmosphere. The bridge over Warner Street, on Rosebery Avenue, is clearly visible on the left and is still a landmark in the area although most of the small streets, courts and yards which were below it have now disappeared. (*Credit: Finsbury Library*)

A GROUP OF COUSINS, ALLOA, FIFE, C. 1905
The level of prosperity achieved by this early date by some of the Italians in Scotland can be seen by the way the children of the Zaccardelli and Iacovelli families, whose parents came from villages in the province of Frosinone, are dressed. Standing, from left to right: Raffaelo Iacovelli, Angelina Iacovelli, Beniamino Zaccardelli and Alberto Zaccardelli. Seated, from left to right are the Iacovelli siblings: Alfonso, Guilietta and Alfredo. The mothers of the group were two of three sisters who came to Scotland in the 1890s after a spell in France as silk-weavers. When the sisters settled in Scotland, all three married men from their province of origin. The families' economic success derived from ice-cream parlours and cafés in the Fife area. (*Credit: M. Renucci*)

BIAGI CHILDREN, BARGA, 1901
Left to right: Augusto, Teresa and Ugo. Much of the emigration at this time was from tiny mountain hamlets rather than the little towns and villages which formed the main or market town of the *comune*. In the *comune* of Barga, for example, migrants came from Sommacolonia, Renaio, Tiglio, Rebosciole. The people who lived in Barga itself were normally better-off than those from the more remote hamlets. This was the case with the Biagi children. They lived in Barga and their parents never emigrated. Nor did Augusto or Ugo. Teresa, born in 1896, however, became engaged to a boy who had decided to emigrate to Scotland. He went over first, and later called for her, in 1920, when he had found accommodation and employment in the business of a fellow *Barghigiano*. Teresa's wedding took place in Glasgow. (*Credit: P. Marchetti*)

THE RENUCCI FAMILY, GLASGOW, C. 1905

Giovanni Renucci was born in Rebosciole, *comune* of Barga (Lu), in 1875. When he was in his early teens he was 'brought' to Glasgow to work for the Giuliani family, the famous *Barghigiani padroni* tycoons who by the turn of the century had a chain of over 60 shops and cafés in the city. After several years working and later managing Giuliani shops, by 1895, at the age of just 20, Giovanni established his own business, 'The Renucci Bakery'. This operation prospered and by the 1930s had also become an importer and wholesaler of Italian wines and provisions, with seven delivery vans supplying shops across the city. After the war, the bakery and provisions side of the business continued in the hands of the eldest son Freddy, standing at the back between his parents; it continued to trade until its closure in 1978. (*Credit: M. Renucci*)

THE PACITTI FAMILY, MOSCOW, 1909

This family emigrated from San Biagio (Fr) to Russia at the end of the nineteenth century. When the revolution came in 1917, they had to flee and returned briefly to Italy. Just after the First World War, however, they left their village again and followed a well-worn path from those parts to Glasgow. Only Caterina, on the right, who was born in Moscow, is still alive. Alessandro, on his father's knee, also born in Moscow, was a survivor of the *Arandora Star* and died aged 86 in February 1991. He was still working in 1990 and was the oldest ice-cream van driver in Glasgow. (*Credit: G. Pacitti*)

ANGELO AND ANNUNZIATA CONETTA, EARLY 1900s
Born in the 1880s in Perella, *comune* of Picinisco (Fr), this couple had an interesting migratory history. In the 1890s Angelo emigrated to America. In the early 1900s he returned to Perella, married Annunziata, here shown wearing the *Ciociaria* costume, and took his bride back to Port Chester, New York, where he had established himself as foreman in an ice factory. Annunziata ran a boarding house and two of their seven children were born there. When the First World War came, the family returned to Italy, Angelo to do his military service. The couple remained in their native hamlet a while, three more children were born and in 1920 they emigrated again — to Glasgow, where Angelo had a brother, already established in a café business. Another two children were born there. These descendants now have links, through marriage, to a large network of the most prominent Italian families in central Scotland. (*Credit: People's Palace Museum*)

EYRE STREET, THE ITALIAN COLONY, LONDON, 1900s
The old Italian quarter was centred around Hatton Garden and Wall. When Clerkenwell Road was opened in 1878, forged through the middle of the Colony between Gray's Inn Road and Farringdon Road, the Colony became known as the 'Clerkenwell Italian Colony'. To the north of the new road was a maze of small streets such as Back Hill, Little Bath Street, Little Saffron Hill as well as Eyre Street and Summers Street, pictured here. To the south of Clerkenwell Road were Hatton Garden and Wall, Leather Lane and Portpool Lane. There was a gradual clearance of the area but it was not until the 1950s that most of the housing disappeared and most of the Italians moved either further north to Islington or elsewhere in the city. Old London Italians still fondly recall life in the Colony where a high percentage of residents were Italian and where there was a great sense of community. (*Credit: E. Salvoni*)

ANNO 1. NUM. 4.   LONDRA: SABATO, 9 OTTOBRE, 1909.   ESCE OGNI SABATO.

L'ITALIANO

ABBONAMENTI:
Regno Unito. Estero.
Trimestre ... 2/- Trimestre Lit. 3.90
Semestre ... 3/6 Semestre „ 6.90
Anno ... ... 6/6 Anno „ 12.50

Per le inserzioni (piccola pubblicità, avvisi commerciali, annunzi, comunicati, ecc) prezzi da convenirsi.
Rivolgersi all' Amministrazione:
15, Bryan Place, Islington, London, N.

1d.   GIORNALE DELLA COLONIA ITALIANA IN LONDRA.   1d

DIRETTORE: DR. G. VASSALLO.

High Class Printing
is essential to a High Class Hotel or Restaurant If yours does not give satisfaction, send us a postcard and our representative will visit you with specimens & sample prices

C. J. BARRETT & SON
— PRINTERS & STATIONERS, —
15, Bryan Place, Islington, London, N.

PASSATO E FUTURO.

È tutto un intrigo fosco e tristo, una matassa arruffatissima che a stento pochissimi potrebbero disciogliere e venirne a capo. Sono sette anni di storia degradante, che ha non solo nociuto fortissimamente a questa povera Società di M. S. fra Impiegati d' Albergo e Ristorante, nel cui seno s' è svolta, ma le cui conseguenze si sono ripercosse su tutta la colonia, poichè ha toccato nomi d' uomini privati e pubblici e pure altre associazioni coloniali specchiatissime. Sono sette anni di storia che noi rifuggiamo dal rievocare siccome alla nostra mente ripugna di rievocare un incubo; è una storia le cui pagine non vorremo, non peranco sfogliare, ma toccare, siccome proviamo ribrezzo di posare la mano su una piaga schifosissima.

Colpa di chi ?

A chi ne risale la responsabilità ?

Nè a uno, nè a due, nè a un numero determinato di persone ; forse

capirebbe poco o nulla, e se ci capisse qualche cosa avrebbe allora il dolore di vedere svelati innanzi a sè fatti e cose che gli farebbero perdere completamente la fede nei suoi fratelli e in sè stesso e a lui verrebbe tale uno scoramento che lo farebbe dubitare dell' avvenire.

Seppelliamo il passato—e volesse il Cielo che la pietra tumulare potesse coprire anche l'odio e la discordia.

Una parola, chè sarà conforto ed esortazione insieme, noi rivolgiamo a quelli che si sentono e veramente sono ingiuriati da quel passato, e che pure non trovano chi simpatizzi con loro o chi li aiuti, poichè hanno bisogno d' aiuti : l'avvenire !

È questo cui dobbiamo volgere il nostro sguardo attento, vigile, ansioso.

Ma pure esso è apparecchiato dal presente.

Noi vediamo un' associazione, una vecchia associazione coloniale, il cui programma è quanto si può desiderare. di più commendevole ed di più giusto, minata nelle sue fondamenta.

E quest' associazione è nonpertanto

per vendetta personale, travisò i fatti veri e verniciandoli d'uno strato lucido, abbagliante, gridò loro : Aiutateci a migliorare e difenderci. In secondo luogo, che scopo diretto, personale, ci domandiamo noi, potrebbero avere i padroni nel distruggere una Società di lavoratori subalterni ?

Certamente è in loro il torto d'avere prestato facile orecchio a quelle insinuazioni e di essersi fatti spingere giù per la china dell' errore fino a usare tutta l'influenza e autorità di cui dispongono per schiacciare la Società vittima : e, ancora più, fino a rendersi complici, forse involontarî, di chi con arti diaboliche e a solo scopo di tornaconto finanziario non si pèrita di cooperarsi all' abbattimento di una Società di mutuo soccorso, colla menzogna e col raggiro.

Pure è innegabile che oggi i padroni, sia agendo personalmente sia concedendo ad altri di usare il loro nome, si sono schierati contro questa Società di mutuo soccorso fra lavoratori colla tenace intenzione di distruggerla. Ed è così che oggi la quistione,

Ma allo stesso tempo non possiamo fare a meno di dire ai lavoratori : unitevi, siate compatti e resistete a questo comando capriccioso che i padroni v' hanno lanciato, e che nuoce non solo ai vostri interessi, ma alla vostra dignità d' uomini liberi.

Voi uniti rappresentate una forza cento volte superiore a quella dei padroni, dai quali non avete nulla a temere. Vi scacceranno dalle loro case, rifiuteranno il vostro lavoro, perchè ricorreranno ad altre braccia —ma sarà per poco, perchè quelle altre braccia apparterranno a uomini che sono compagni vostri, fratelli vostri, i quali si rifiuteranno quindi di prestarsi a quel lavoro che sarà per loro odioso.

Siate compatti e guardate sempre dritto nella via che avete da percorrere, senza timori e preoccupazioni.

I padroni oppongono alla vostra un' altra società, ove si raduna la crème dei lavoratori d' albergo e ristorante, dove convengono i chefs, i maître d' hôtel, i direttori, loro stessi, i padroni ? Lasciate che vi sia opposta

L'ITALIANO, LONDON, 1909

There were many early attempts at launching and sustaining Community newspapers, especially in London, but also in the smaller provincial Colonies of Manchester and Glasgow. Most, however, had short life spans not lasting more than a few years. (*Credit: British Museum*)

ANNO I   GLASGOW Venerdì 7 Febbraio 1908   NUMERO 5

LA SCOZIA

Organo settimanale per gl'interessi della Colonia italiana

Si pubblica tutti i VENERDI. – Un numero separato 1d, arretrato 2d

PREZZO
INSERZIONI
Pag. IV un quarta di uguale a due pagine per 2e mezzo
ANNO   £ 5 5
SEMESTRE £ 3 3
TRIMESTRE £ 2 0
UNA VOLTA   4/-
III Per seduta di linea   9d
„ II   „   6d
„ I   „   3d
Quattro inserzioni consecutive per il prezzo di tre

LA SCOZIA Publishing C°.
PROPRIETARIA
I manoscritti non pubblicati non si restituiscono.

ABBONAMENTI
PER UN ANNO (52 num.) 6s 6d --- PER SEI MESI (26 num.) 3s 3d
PER TRE MESI (13 num.) 1s 8d
FRANCO A DOMICILIO

DIREZIONE E AMMINISTRAZIONE
71 Dundas Street
Prof. FILIPPO CAFARO Direttore

PREZZO
RATE
for
ADVERTISEMENTS
Page IV 2 x 2½ inch. space
„ 1 year   £ 5 5
„ half year £ 3 3
„ quarter   £ 2
„ week   4/-
PAGE III every space of a inch
PAGE II   1/-
PAGE I   1/6
Four consecutive insertions for the price of three.

Per la Scuola Italiana
POSSIBILE O IMPOSSIBILE?

Giovedì 6 febbraio

Quei pochi che vivamente s'interessano del continuo progredire della nostra Colonia in coro mi gridano con un certo rammarico: È impossiblie, è impossibile! Ed io cocciuto come un mulo, stretto nella mia ferma convinzione, col carico del grave progetto della Scuola sul dorso, cerco sempre di andare innanzi nella scabrosa via e di mostrare a tutti gl'increduli, ai diffidenti, ed agli scoraggiti che la fondazione della scuola è cosa di

mesi di strenuo lavoro dovette rinunziare alla nobile intrapresa per gli ostacoli insormontabili che si frapposero. Facemmo scomodare persino S. E. l'Arcivescovo di Glasgow, ma non ci fu caso; tutto fu impossibile, e crediamo che sia tuttora impossibile. - Quattro anni fa? Adunque avete in tutto questo lungo periodo dormito tranquillamente sui soffici cuscini di questa dannosa credenza, di questa malaugurata convinzione, senza studiarvi di trovare nuove vie e nuovi

Il congresso degl'italiani all'estero

Dalla Tribuna del 29 gennaio u° s. rileviamo:

Il Comitato direttivo del Congresso degli italiani all'estero, indetto per l'ottobre 1908 in Roma, ha preso le seguenti deliberazioni, nella sua seduta del 10 dicembre, in merito alla formazione del Congresso stesso:

1) Il Congresso del 1908, aperto a tutte le attività e a tutte le manifestazioni che possano portare più utile contributo ai suoi lavori, lasciando al Congresso del 1911 quei

"Atti" ed alle altre pubblicazioni ufficiali del Congresso ed alla medaglia commemorativa-

Già sono in corso con le Compagnie di Navigazione, con le Ferrovie dello Stato, con l'Associazione pel Movimento dei forestieri e con l'Associazione degli albergatori, trattative per ottenere speciali ribassi e facilitazioni non solo per i viaggi marittimi e terrestri, ma anche per alloggi, gite, ecc. a favore dei congressisti.

Una o due sedute finali del Congresso, che avrà il suo svolgimento in Roma, saranno per speciali accordi presi col Comitato dell'Espo-

LA SCOZIA, GLASGOW, 1906

La Scozia was concerned with many issues which affected the Community. A highlight in 1906 was the visit of the Italian Ambassador to the Scottish Italian Community. This was given extensive coverage in *La Scozia*. Despite widescale advertising by the Italians, production of the newspaper only lasted one year. (*Credit: Mitchell Library*)

THE PROCESSION OF THE *MADONNA DEL CARMINE*, LONDON, EARLY 1900s

The *Madonna* first left St Peter's Italian Church in a glorious procession in 1883 and was the first Catholic procession of this type in Britain since the Reformation. The procession always takes place on the first Sunday after 6 July. Although the statue is not visible in this photograph, the festival atmosphere in Clerkenwell, then still very much an Italian Colony, is captured with the old monarchist Italian flags and banners draped from the houses and the throng of those following the procession below in the street. (*Credit: La Voce*)

THE *MADONNA DEL ROSARIO*, WHIT WALK, MANCHESTER, C. 1905

The Manchester Italian Catholic Society was founded in 1889. In 1890 the Italians of Ancoats took part in their first Whit Walk, proudly bearing the *Madonna* of the Rosary, encircled in white lilies. Unlike the procession of the *Madonna del Carmine* in London, which is exclusively an Italian feast day, the Manchester procession comprises English 'walkers' from many of the city's Catholic parishes and schools. (*Credit: A. Rea*)

CHAPTER THREE

The 1910s

During this decade, many Italians really began to prosper. The most intelligent and entrepreneurial pioneers, who had struck out on their own and seized opportunities, were now beginning to reap substantial profits. As *padroni*, they continued to bring over new migrants. Many people, however, as a result of their hard work over many years and economical living, had now accumulated enough money to achieve their dream of returning home to Italy as prosperous men and women. Their return, of course, provided a further incentive for others to try to follow in their footsteps. Not quite so literally any more, as a number now travelled by train, and some by sea.

The First World War caused a disruption to the way of life in the British Italian Community as it did for most people throughout Europe. However, it did not wreak anything like the havoc on the Community that the Second World War brought simply because Italy and Great Britain, fortunately, were allies. When Italy entered the war in 1915, there was a strong patriotic response and over 8,000 Italian men left Britain to return to Italy to fight for their country. After the war, many men returned to Britain as heroes, bearing military honours for bravery. However, before returning to Britain, it was common for the soldiers, particularly those who had distinguished themselves in the war, to choose Italian wives from their villages to join them abroad. Many young British-born members of the second generation of Italian migrants fought during the First World War in the British Armed Forces.

The embryonic catering industry continued to grow, particularly in London where the second Italian Colony, in Soho, really began to flourish. The Italians in Soho were rather different from those in Clerkenwell. They often came from the north of Italy, especially Piemonte, and Lombardia, and were employed in the kitchens of the hotels, clubs and restaurants of the West End. They saw themselves as a cut above the Clerkenwell Italians since they were often better paid and worked in the more sophisticated environment 'up West'.

In Manchester's Ancoats and in Clerkenwell, the ice-cream makers continued to live and work within the Colony and sell their product by means of push-barrows and horses and carts. However, it was elsewhere in the country, surprisingly in the colder north, in Scotland, but perhaps more predictably in coastal locations, that the ice-cream parlours, and the small cafés with their trade centred on ice-cream, began to proliferate. In London also, individual Italians opened up small businesses of their own, selling snacks, confectionery and tobacco.

After more than a generation of immigration, having surmounted many of the initial problems, having settled into the economic and social structure in this country, by the end of the First World War, a new and golden era was about to dawn for the British Italian Community.

TWO MAGNIFICENT D'ORAZIO ICE-CREAM WAGONS READY TO LEAVE FROM THE ITALIAN COLONY, LONDON, C. 1910

By this date the ice-cream industry in London was well organised. The main producers all had their own territories and the problems of hygiene were overcome with the introduction of the ice-cream cone. These wagons would be drawn to particular sites early in the morning and left for a day's trading — extra supplies of ice-cream were brought from base if required. Boys were employed as 'runners', relaying orders for more ice-cream back to the manufacturing operation which, in the case of a firm the size of D'Orazio, had long since moved from the domestic kitchen to a production base. (*Credit: La Voce*)

'PURE ICES' WAGON, A LONDON PARK, C. 1910

Displaying British and Italian flags at the front, this elaborate wagon, with its staff of four, would have been horse-drawn and sited strategically for the day's business. The lady's *Ciociaria* costume indicates her origin in the Frosinone province; the tin on the counter, containing cones, tells us that the era of the 'licking glass' is now over. (*Credit: La Voce*)

THE FIRST SERVINI PROVISIONS SHOP, MOUNT PLEASANT, NEAR CLERKENWELL, LONDON, 1912
Opened by Pietro and Domenico Servini who arrived in London from Vallora, Varsi (Pr) in 1902, father and son worked in the kitchens of Soho before setting up their shop supplying the Italian Community. At this time the other Italian suppliers to the Colony were Gazzani, Mariani and Terroni. In 1929, the shop moved to King's Cross, its new location reflecting the movement north out of the Colony by many Italians. It remained there for 42 years when, in the hands of Domenico's son-in-law, who had taken over in 1964, it moved to its third location, in Caledonian Road, where it traded until 1984. The fourth generation, nine in number, are mainly professionals, and none now remain in the shop tradition. (*Credit: G. Giacon*)

CARLO TIANI AND HIS SON NATALINO OUTSIDE THEIR PROVISIONS SHOP, ANCOATS, MANCHESTER, 1913
Carlo, from Sette Fratte (Fr), had arrived in Manchester in 1878, starting out as an organ grinder. By 1913 he had become a *padrone*, importing boys from his village for his growing business empire. As well as the shop, which supplied all Italian household needs (note the shawls draped over the back of the window display), he made ice-cream and owned a number of barrows with which he sent the boys out daily. He also owned and managed a number of barrel organs. Natalino is wearing the uniform of the *Bersaglieri* Boys' Band which was founded in Manchester by Domenico Antonelli in 1912. (*Credit: A. Rea*)

THE GONNELLA CAFÉ, GLASGOW, 1915
The Gonnella family from Barga (Lu) were amongst the first to settle permanently in Scotland, having come initially on a temporary basis as statuette sellers. By the 1880s they and other families began to move into the catering trades, as street-sellers, and eventually were able to establish permanent premises such as the one pictured here. (*Credit: P. Cresci*)

GONNELLA AND CASCI, GLASGOW, 1919

The Gonnella family entered into partnership with the Casci family, another old and well known Barga family who had been migrating, like Gonnella, to Chicago since 1850 as *figurinai* and some of whom, again like Gonnella, had eventually settled in Glasgow. Many young boy and girl workers, as shown here, were brought over from Barga to staff their shops. The young workers hoped one day to open their own shop. (*Credit: P. Cresci*)

DI MAMBRO & CO., PORTH, RHONDDA, 1919

Shortly after his wedding in 1918, Carmino Di Mambro set up his business in Porth. His venture prospered and throughout the 1920s he was able to send a little money home to his parents and siblings in Italy, who never emigrated, in addition to looking after his own growing family in this country. This photograph and the previous page illustrate the similarities in style between the Scottish and the Welsh Italian café in this era. (*Credit: A. Bacchetta*)

A LARGE CROWD OF ITALIANS GATHER AT GREAT ANCOATS STREET WHEN ITALY ENTERS THE FIRST WORLD WAR, MANCHESTER, 1915

British and Italian flags flew in unison and levels of patriotism ran high within the Italian Communities up and down the country. Over 8,000 Italian men resident in Britain returned to Italy for military service. They served on the Austrian front and were often awarded the *Croce di Guerra*, returning to Britain in 1919 as heroes. (*Credit: A. Rea*)

A HUGE CROWD OF ITALIANS GATHER AT PICCADILLY WHEN ITALY ENTERS THE FIRST WORLD WAR, LONDON, 1915

In the car are the *Ex Garibaldini* Stinghi, Geloso and Francesco Saccotelli, by this time in their eighties. Over 170 men of the London Italian Community, as well as others from elsewhere in Great Britain, lost their lives fighting in the Italian forces in the First World War. There is a monument to these soldiers at the Italian Church in London, and, until its closure, there was also a plaque at the *Casa d'Italia* in Glasgow to commemorate the Glasgow Italians who were lost. (*Credit: La Voce*)

ITALIAN SOLDIERS ON THE AUSTRO-ITALIAN BORDER, 1916
All seven of these men came from Manchester's 'Little Italy', Ancoats. Vincenzo Schiavo is seated second from the left and also in the group are a Rossi, a Quiligotti, a Mancini and a Longinotti. After the war, a marble stone was placed in Peter's Square in Manchester, alongside the British First World War Memorial, to commemorate the Italian allies who were also lost in the war. This stone was removed during the Second World War and replaced only in 1990. (*Credit A. Rea*)

EMIDIO AND ALFONSO CROLLA FROM THE EDINBURGH ITALIAN COMMUNITY, 1915
The brothers were born in Picinisco (Fr) in the 1880s and arrived in Edinburgh around the turn of the century. Their first café business was in Easter Road. During the First World War they returned to Italy to fight for their country and returned safely to Edinburgh after the war. By 1925, with Valvona, also from Picinisco, they had established their famous Provisions Store, which is still in operation today. Alfonso Crolla was very active within the Italian Community and was awarded the *Cavaliere* by the Italian government. Sadly, he lost his life during the Second World War, when the *Arandora Star*, transporting Italian internees to Canada, was torpedoed in the Irish Sea. (*Credit: People's Palace Museum*)

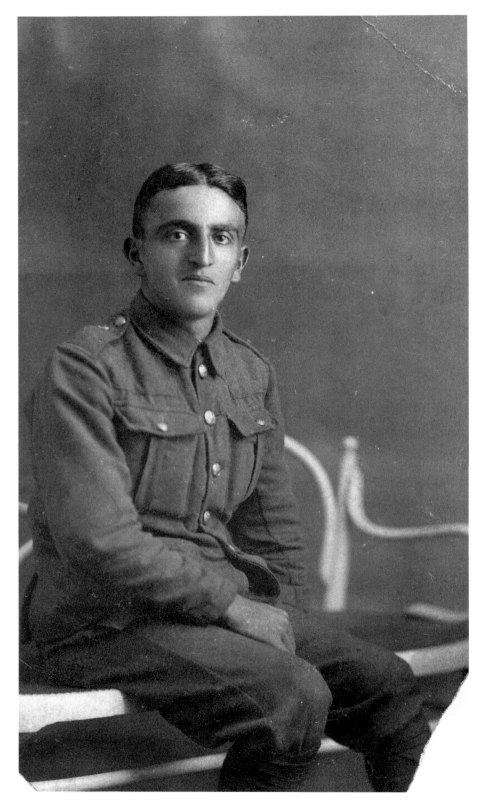

**LUIGI ARCARI, BRITISH ARMY SOLDIER, FIRST
WORLD WAR**
British-born second generation Italians were also
drafted into the British army during the First
World War. When one family had men serving
in both the British and the Italian Army, there
was no conflict — such difficulties were to come
later in the Second World War. (*Credit: A. Arcari
Pollard*)

GIUSEPPE DE LUCIO, ITALIAN ARMY SOLDIER, FIRST
WORLD WAR
(*Credit: D. De Marco Cullen*)

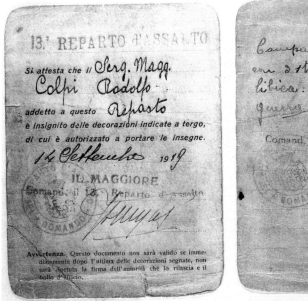 

FIRST WORLD WAR DECORATION, *CROCE DI GUERRA*, OF SERGEANT MAJOR RODOLFO COLPI
The decoration was awarded to Rodolfo Colpi in 1916 at Gargersch when he fought as an *arditto*
on the Austrian front. After the war he returned to Gourock where he had lived since emigrating
from the Val di Vara (Sp) in 1909. (*Credit: R. Colpi*)

LUIGI SERAFINI AND ISABELLA MOSCONI, BARGA, 1918
Serafini emigrated to Scotland in the 1890s, as one of a group of four brothers, at the age of 12.
He had done very well in Hawick and after the First World War and service in the Italian Army,
he returned to Barga (Lu) as a prosperous man to choose a wife. Isabella Mosconi, a school
teacher, from Florence, returned with him to Scotland and found the life of the emigrant *Barghigi-ani* in those days to be rather different from the lifestyle she had enjoyed as a teacher in Italy.
(*Credit: R. Serafini*)

CARMINO DI MAMBRO AND DOMENICA TAMBINI, PONTYPRIDD, RHONDDA, 1918
Carmino Di Mambro, born in 1883, walked with his brother from their native Rocca Monfina (Ce) to London in the 1890s. There they worked as 'ice men', delivering blocks of ice with a horse and cart around the hotels, restaurants and ice-cream makers of the Italian Colony. By 1915, however, he had arrived in Wales and in 1918 he married Domenica Tambini; the couple are pictured here on their wedding day. Domenica was born in Grezzo in the *comune* of Bardi (Pr) in 1890. The couple had one daughter and five sons, one of whom, Bert Di Mambro, now lives in Merthyr Tydfil and is active in the *Amici Val Ceno Galles* Association (See also bottom photo on p. 38). (*Credit: B. Di Mambro*)

SISTERS ELVIRA DEL CIPRESSO AND MARIA FAFONDI, ABERDEEN, 1913
Elvira, seated on the left, had recently been widowed. She had emigrated from Novigena in the Val di Vara (Sp) with her husband in the early 1900s and by 1912 had become so prosperous that they built a villa in their village — testimony to their success. The loss of her husband in 1912 was a blow to Elvira who sent for her sister Maria Fafondi (both née Nardi) to come to Aberdeen and take her children, Anna and Giuseppe, back to Italy. Alone, she was unable to carry on the business and look after the children too. The arrival of Maria in Aberdeen merited a family portrait, taken at a studio in Market Street, before the family split up again. Anna and Giuseppe spent the next 12 years growing up in Italy. They returned to Scotland in 1925, by which time their mother had remarried. (The girl at the back is unknown.) (*Credit: A. Dorà*)

THE ROSSI 'FAMILY', GREENOCK, 1915
Standing at the back in the middle is Davide Rossi who was born in Stagnedo in the *comune* of Beverino (Sp) in 1876. In the 1890s, he walked through France and England, finally settling in Gourock on the Clyde Coast. By the early 1900s he had three shops and, as a *padrone*, sent for young boys and girls from his village to come and work for him. Apart from his wife Albina, seated at the front with daughter Ancella on her lap (who is still living in Glasgow today), the other adults pictured here all worked for Davide Rossi. Seated on the extreme left is Silvia Lodola and, on the right Linda Lodola, her sister. Standing at the back on the left is Realdo Ciuffardi and on the right Pasquale Pattucci. Davide brought at least six other young people from Stagnedo and Padivarma before the premature death of both himself and his wife in 1919 of Spanish flu. The embryonic empire thus folded and Ancella, Lina and brothers Dorlindo and Oliver were sent back to relatives in Italy before themselves returning to Scotland in the 1920s.
(*Credit: A. Rossi Chiocconi*)

THREE OF FIVE GIULIANOTTI SIBLINGS, FRASERBURGH, ABERDEENSHIRE, 1914

From left to right: Giulia, Maria Delina and Roberto. Maria Delina married Emilio Bicocchi in 1917 when she was 18 years of age and moved to Peterhead. Later the family moved again, to Aberdeen, where her son, Edwin Bicocchi, remains today, proprietor of the Premier Grill Restaurant in Market Square, an area which for many years was the centre of Aberdeen's Italian Community. (*Credit: E. Bicocchi*)

FAMILY ZANRÈ, BORGO VAL DI TARO (PR), 1918

Standing, from left to right: 'Jock' Zanrè, his son Luigi, an unknown lady, son Giovanni and daughter Tina. Seated, Jock's wife, Assunta Bicocchi, with daughter Marietta on her lap. From Val Dena, a small hamlet in the *comune* of Borgo Val di Taro, Jock emigrated at the turn of the century, in his pre-marital days, to Peterhead, in Aberdeenshire, where he spent several years working before returning to Italy. In 1920, however, Luigi at the age of 16, returned to Peterhead to join an uncle. Later he moved to Huntly and finally settled in London, where his two sons Ronaldo and Bruno still live today. (*Credit: E. Bicocchi*)

THE WEDDING OF LUIGI ARCARI AND GIULIA DE MARCO, EDINBURGH, 1915
Both of these families originated in the province of Frosinone but the Arcari family settled in Glasgow and the De Marco family in Portobello on the east coast. There are in fact almost equal contingents of people who originate in Frosinone living in Glasgow and Edinburgh and there is much social interaction between the two groups. The couple behind the bride, on her right, are Gabriele and Cristina De Marco who owned the famous Maison De Marco on Portobello Pier, an enormous restaurant-café of outstanding beauty as well as a great centre of entertainment with its own orchestra and cabaret shows. The name the couple gave to their restaurant, *Maison*, indicates a French influence which had been acquired by the family during its migration to France prior to arrival in Scotland. (*Credit: A. Arcari Pollard*)

CHAPTER FOUR

The 1920s and The 1930s

The 1920s and the 1930s were something of a golden era for the Italians in Great Britain. It was in these two decades, after a generation of settlement, that the Community reached a maturity, a stability and an increasing economic prosperity. All of this afforded an increasing respectability — a place in society. The number of self-employed grew substantially in this era and thus continued to insulate the Community from the trauma of unemployment suffered by so many in Britain in the Depression of the 1930s.

There were, however, restrictions in this period, at both ends of the 'chain'. Firstly, the Aliens Order of 1920 restricted immigration, so that only people who had a work permit could enter Britain. For the prospective migrant, a work permit could only be secured if one had family or *paesani* in Britain prepared to make the necessary application to the Ministry of Labour. Secondly, in Italy the new fascist government in the late 1920s and 1930s was keen to check the flow of so many young, fit and ambitious Italians out of the country.

Many people, however, did succeed in entering Britain in this era, especially boys drafted into the kitchens of the growing number of Italian-owned restaurants in Soho, but also people who came to work for family businesses up and down the country. The chains of migration, which were very well established by now, were resilient and persistent. The role of the *padrone* continued, particularly in the small businesses of the north of England, Wales and Scotland where, because more and more people were succeeding in opening up their own shops, a constant stream of new workers was always needed. Boys and family members who had been brought as staff most often had to move, to seek a new territory, when the time came for them to open their own shop. By hard, steady and dedicated work, a good living could be made. In London, many small fortunes had already been acquired.

A number of trades and occupations, established in the last century, continued to flourish, notably the *arrotini*, or knife grinders, who by the 1920s had also become cutlery makers; the ice men; the mosaic and *terrazzo* workers; the asphalters, and in London the statuette makers. There was a sense of security and of future prosperity in the Community. A way of life which supported the family, and offered levels of prosperity unknown in Italy, had been found. The future was full of hope, especially for the young and the aspirant.

The most significant development within the Italian Community in the 1930s was something quite different: the rise of fascism. The movement grew, as it did in Italy, based in Britain upon the *ex combattenti*, the men who had fought for Italy in the First World War and who were seen by the Italian authorities as true Italian patriots. For most of the rank-and-file Italians in Britain, in fact, support for fascism was seen as normal patriotism. The growth and organisation of the *fasci*, or fascist clubs, across the country was rapid and represented the first attempt by the Italian State to draw together the straggling and neglected Italian Communities throughout the world. The *fasci* offered a wide range of social activities including trips to Italy for the children of members. The majority of British Italians were happy to be involved, little realising the consequences that such association would shortly bring.

By 1939, and the outbreak of the Second World War, the Italians resident in Britain had attained a significant level of economic prosperity and a considerable degree of social integration and respectability. It had been a golden era, but it was coming to an end.

A. CANALE WITH HIS ICE-CREAM BARROW AT CWMPARC, RHONDDA, 1924
The Italians settled in Wales in the 1880s and 1890s, dispersing mainly from London. A large number were from the Val Ceno and particularly the *comune* of Bardi (Pr). As in Scotland, they spread out, in this case across the Welsh valleys, with one or two families establishing themselves in each small town. In this era cones cost a half-penny and wafers a penny. (*Credit: C. Batstone*)

T. TORTELLO WITH HIS ICE-CREAM HORSE AND CART OUTSIDE HIS SHOP, CWMPARC, RHONDDA, 1924
Italian cafés became convivial meeting places in the Rhondda and regardless of the name above the door, all became known as 'Bracchi's'. Giulio Bracchi from Bardi (Pr) was the first man to open a café in Tonypandy, Rhondda, in the 1890s; soon he had three cafés, three Bracchi's. Henceforth, all Italian businesses were known as Bracchi's. *Signor* Tortello, pictured here, was a keen football fan and in the Depression days he bought the first set of jerseys for Cwmparc Football Club. (*Credit: C. Batstone*)

BENITO SCAPPATICCI WITH HIS ICE-CREAM BARROW, PICCADILLY, MANCHESTER, LATE 1930s
One of three brothers from Santo Padre (Fr), Benito, or Bernard as he was known, Scappaticci came to Manchester in the late 1880s. The ice-cream business had been set up there by his elder brother, Girolamo, the first to arrive — via the London Italian Community — and who 'called for' his two younger brothers, Benito and Angelo, who came directly to Ancoats in Manchester. The Scappaticci family acquired the central pitches in Manchester for their barrows. Today, the grandson of Benito, Bernard Scappaticci, carries on in the business founded by his grandfather. Still called 'Ben's Ices', he has three ice-cream vans which operate in the centre of Manchester. (*Credit: B. Scappaticci*)

AN ICE-CREAM SELLER, SAFFRON HILL, LONDON, 1922
We cannot tell what the joke was, but we can see clearly how the ice-cream was transported to, and conserved at its point of sale. Clearly the man with the little notebook is receiving a supply of ice-cream to replenish his stock. The zinc containers inside the wooden barrels held the ice-cream, the space between the two being packed with ice and salt which created a brine, maintaining the ice-cream at the correct temperature. The barrel in the middle is the new one, the container full of ice-cream is securely fastened and held upright in the barrel. The barrel on the right, over which some discussion is taking place, is empty (or almost!) and ready to go back to base. (*Credit: Hulton Picture Library*)

ARTURO GIULIANOTTI ON HIS ICE-CREAM MOTOR BIKE, STONEHAVEN, ABERDEENSHIRE, 1933
The hand-pushed barrows were often replaced by tricycles, with the chest for the container of ice-cream positioned at the front of the cycle. The tricycles were heavy and rather difficult to steer. Here, Arturo Giulianotti, who is still alive and who, with his wife, runs the newsagents in Stonehaven, has devised an ingenious contraption, the 'Ice-Cream Motor Bike'.
(*Credit: E. Bicocchi*)

ZANRÈ ICE-CREAM CAR, HUNTLY, ABERDEENSHIRE, 1930S
By the 1930s, especially in Scotland, ice-cream was being transported in a range of vehicles. In the more sparsely populated areas of the country mobility between markets was essential. In addition to his magnificent car, Luigi Zanrè proudly announces that his ice-cream is made by machine — no more hand turning! (*Credit: R. Zanrè*)

BAR ITALIA AND BIANCHI'S RESTAURANT, FRITH STREET, SOHO, 1930s
The Soho Italian Colony had grown steadily from the turn of the century. By the 1920s and 1930s the first of the Italian restaurants began to open. Bianchi's, so named after the owner, opened in 1928 and quickly became popular with actors, artists and writers. Bar Italia was also owned by the Bianchi family until after the Second World War. Bianchi's finally closed in the 1980s, but Bar Italia is still in business and very popular with young Italians today. (*Credit: E. Salvoni*)

THREE YOUNG WAITERS FROM GENNARO'S RESTAURANT, LONDON, 1928
One of the grand old Italian restaurants of Soho in this era, Gennaro's employed a large staff of boys recruited by the local Italian family networks of chain migration. Many were brought over as young as 12 to work in the kitchens. At this time Gennaro's had no alcohol licence, so one of their jobs was to fetch drinks from the pub next door. Naturally the boys aimed to learn English and be allowed into the dining rooms in order to climb up the ladder, from general hand to *commis* waiter, to waiter and then to head waiter. From this position, they might aspire to become a proprietor, perhaps in partnership with a colleague. Many succeeded.
(*Credit: G. Guarnieri*)

THE SOHO WAITERS RACE, LONDON, 1932
This race, first run in the 1920s, was popular amongst West End waiters, who were almost exclusively Italian in this era. The tradition continued until the 1970s. In action here at Paddington Park are the team from the Café Royal. During the 1930s waiters at the Café Royal earned very little and had to bear the full cost of any breakages in the kitchens, as well as the dining rooms. In addition, tips had to be given over to the head waiter who then made a distribution to the waiters, leaving little for the *commis* waiters and general hands. The Waiters Race was always seen as a great diversion. (*Credit: G. Guarnieri*)

AN 'ICE MAN', LONDON, 1920

Before the advent of refrigeration the ice men performed a vital role within the embryonic catering trade, especially for ice-cream. Initially the ice was cut from glaciers in Norway and transported up the Thames to river-side underground cold storage rooms. From here the ice men, with horse and cart, would deliver blocks of ice to hotels, restaurants and ice-cream makers across the city. Once delivered, there was a range of hand-turned machinery available, such as ice breakers and crushers, to break up the large blocks. (*Credit: La Voce*)

ICE MEN, CARLO GATTI ICE COMPANY, LONDON, 1921

The staff of the Battersea Depot, about to set out on a jaunt to Hastings. By the 1930s, ice was produced by refrigeration and, as more and more catering establishments introduced their own fridges, the demand for the ice declined. Also, belt driven vertical freezers had been invented to produce ice-cream using compressed brine rather than ice to maintain temperatures. By the late 1930s there were only half a dozen Italian ice companies left in London. They were: Gatti, Perella, Bonvini, Biondino, Inzani and Assirati. (*Credit: La Voce*)

KNIFE GRINDERS OR *ARROTINI*, LONDON, 1927

Knife grinding, a specialist and semi-skilled occupation, was conducted exclusively by men from the Val Rendena in Trentino. They arrived in London from the 1870s pushing their *moleta* — a sort of wheelbarrow with the wheel itself being used for knife sharpening — all the way across Europe. London was a rapidly growing city at this time, one of the largest in the world, and the number of catering establishments of all types was also growing. The *arrotini* found a very lucrative niche which they controlled for their *paesani*. The main families of *arrotini* were Collini, Di Prè, Beltrami, Sicheri, Nella, Ferrari and Caola. Many individuals had nicknames to distinguish the members of one family with the same christian and surname. (*Credit: A. Collini*)

LEO MATURI, CUTLERS, BIRMINGHAM, 1930

Several of the *arrotini* families who settled in this country became cutlery makers. The progression from sharpening knives to making knives and other cutlery was a natural one. There were several firms in London in the 1930s, notably Collini and Ferrari. Maturi was the main firm outside London, with branches in Birmingham and Leeds. There was Caola in Bristol and Tisi in Southampton, and Acciari in Aberdeenshire was the only Scottish Italian cutler in the 1930s. Only Ferrari in Soho survives today as a specialist supplier for catering equipment in general. (*Credit: La Voce*)

ANGELO VALLE, MOSAIC WORKER, SHEFFIELD, 1920
Born in Cavasso Nuovo (Pn) in 1896, this man arrived in England at the age of 24 as one of a group of *Friulani* mosaic specialists who were engaged to work at Bebington County Hospital. The document is an 'Aliens Book'. Italians who arrived in Britain after the Aliens Order of 1920 had to register changes of employment and address with the police. From this we can trace the life of Angelo Valle. Throughout the 1920s and 1930s he continued in mosaic work, moving from Liverpool and Sheffield to Manchester and then to Nottingham. On his return from internment on the Isle of Man after the Second World War, however, due to falling demand for his specialist craft, he was reduced to taking up work as a 'concrete worker' in Manchester in 1944. A year later he married an English woman, and in 1952, after more than 30 years in this country, he retired to Italy. (*Credit: Console S. Mercuri*)

VITTORIO SARTOR, MOSAIC WORKER, LONDON, 1920

Vittorio, from Friuli, seen here working at his specialist craft of restoring ancient Roman mosaics, lived in Muswell Hill, London. Such was his reputation in this field he was commissioned, for example, by the British Archaeology Society, 25 years after we see him here, to restore Roman mosaics damaged in the centre of Exeter by German bombing during the Second World War. (*Credit: La Voce*)

SIGNOR GINOCCHIO, WHO WORKED FOR CHIAPPA, PUNCHING A MUSICAL TEXT FOR A BARREL ORGAN, 1920

The production of organs required a variety of skills, most importantly carpentry for making the organ cabinet, and musical composition for the tunes. The best organ makers, like Robino of Manchester, who had trained as a musician in Marseilles, composed their own tunes. The organ contained a wooden cylinder the size of a garden roller over which was fastened the paper with the notes punched out individually to form the tune. As the barrel was turned by the handle, the punched holes would activate the small hammers which struck against the strings producing the notes. The better the organ, the more hammers, since this could produce a wider range of notes. Tunes could be changed regularly by replacing the paper text. (*Credit: Finsbury Library*)

CHIAPPA, ORGAN MAKERS, LONDON, 1924
The Chiappa organ-making firm was founded in 1865 in Clerkenwell by Giuseppe Chiappa and carried on by his sons Carlo, Luigi and Andrea. When organ grinding had declined as an occupation for Italians by the 1900s, the business survived by moving from barrel organs into production and repair of the bigger fairground and show organs which were very popular throughout the 1920s and 1930s. Here, a Marenghi organ, which had been made in Paris and installed at the Dominion Theatre in London, is brought into the Chiappa factory for repair and tuning. On the left is Victor Chiappa, who still looks after the family business in its original premises in Eyre Street Hill. (*Credit: Finsbury Library*)

ZACCARDELLI & CERVI FACTORY WORKERS, EDINBURGH, 1923
Seated in the middle is Sabatino Cervi who was born in Manchester 1890. As a child he returned with his parents to their native Picinisco (Fr) and just after the First World War he returned alone to Manchester as a young man. From there he moved to Edinburgh and went into partnership with Zaccardelli, who had founded a biscuit manufacturing business in 1909, to supply the Italian ice-cream industry in Scotland. The man with the trilby hat standing at the back of the group is Michele Pelosi, also from Manchester, who followed Sabatino Cervi north to Edinburgh to become factory foreman. Today, the company still exists, run by the grandson of the founder, Adolfo Zaccardelli, and the son of Sabatino Cervi, Adolfo Cervi. (*Credit: A. Cervi*)

FACTORY WORKERS STANDING IN FRONT OF ONE OF THE ZACCARDELLI & CERVI DELIVERY VANS, 1923
Michele Pelosi is in the middle at the back. The factory girls and the young men in both photographs are all sons and daughters of Italian immigrants in Edinburgh. (*Credit: A. Cervi*)

ANTONELLI OLIVE OIL LABEL
Domenico Antonelli was born in Picinisco (Fr) in 1857. He emigrated to London in 1880 and by 1894 had moved to Manchester where he established his organ factory (See p. 15.) The business empire of this elder statesman of the Manchester Italian Community also included a hotel, a retail Italian grocery and wholesale wine merchants, and from 1912, a biscuit and cone manufacturing operation supplying the ice-cream industry of the north of England. This business continues today in the hands of third generation Roland Antonelli, now in his 60s.
(*Credit: R. Antonelli*)

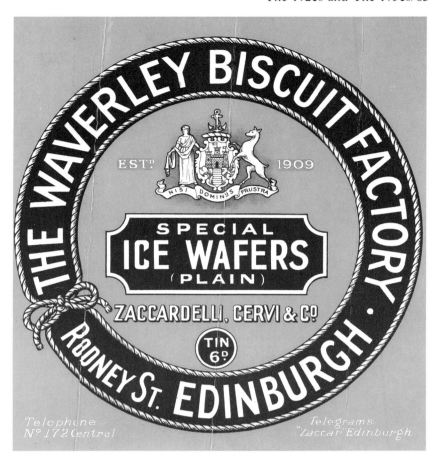

ZACCARDELLI BISCUIT TIN LABEL
In some of the earlier ice-cream photographs (see bottom photo on p. 35, and also p. 53) metal tins of wafers and cones have been visible on the carts and counters. This picture is of one of the paper labels, affixed to the sides of these tins. Nowadays the cones are stored inside plastic bags in cardboard boxes. (*Credit: A. Zaccardelli*)

A RENUCCI BAKERY BREAD-ROLL PAPER BAG
(See top photo on p. 30). (*Credit: M. Renucci*)

THE SABINI GANG, LONDON, 1920S
This gang, the 'Racing Fraternity' as they were known, was centred on the Sabini brothers in Clerkenwell. They controlled race track gambling which in this era was illegal. Bets were taken on street corners by 'bookies' and relayed to the track. The Sabini Gang also 'protected' the Italian Colony in a time when anti-Italian sentiment was prevalent and Italians found it very difficult to find jobs. There was considerable feuding between the Sabini Gang and the Cortesi Gang, another similar group. In an attempted murder of both Sabini brothers, by the three Cortesi brothers, Harry Sabini was shot, and badly wounded, in the *Fratellanza Club* in Clerkenwell in 1922. During the court case the judge praised Luisa Doralli, daughter of the owner of the *Fratellanza*, for her bravery in trying to come between the feuding factions as a human shield. (*Credit: Finsbury Library*)

ASPHALTERS, LONDON, 1936
Large numbers of Italians, particularly those resident in the Clerkenwell Colony, worked as asphalters from the early 1900s and throughout the 1920s and 1930s. This was a heavy labouring job generally undertaken by the poorly educated and unskilled migrants of the Colony. The work was hard, mainly involving roof and road resurfacing, and hours were very long. Most of the asphalters worked on a freelance basis, so employment was not always steady. The role of the 'potter' was one of the toughest; he had to travel to the site and have the pot of asphalt hot and ready for use by 5 a.m. By the 1930s, Ghirardani was the main Italian firm employing asphalters. (*Credit: Finsbury Library*)

THE SCOTIA FISH RESTAURANT, DUNDEE, 1924

The Italian Community in Dundee came mainly from the province of Frosinone, especially the village of Belmonte Castello, with a smaller contingent of the old migrants from the *comune* of Borgo Val di Taro (Pr). Coming as they did almost entirely from poor mountain hamlets where life had been hard and existence precarious, the acquisition of a family business represented an enormous step forward in terms of their economic and social status. In the 1920s and 1930s, it was very common for Italians to be photographed outside their shops, such was their pride in their achievement. (*Credit: La Voce*)

THE PREMIER CAFÉ, GLASGOW, 1930

This splendid example of a 1930s shop belonged to one of the many inter-related Crolla families who had emigrated to Scotland from two hamlets, Fontitune and Valle Porcina in the *comune* of Picinisco from 1880 onwards. High in the Abruzzi mountains, in an area now part of the Abruzzo National Park, these isolated little mountain communities lived entirely on sheep herding. Shown here is the second and third generation of the family — the father who had been born in Glasgow in 1889 and two of his sons. The pride taken in their material advancement, through emigration to Scotland and decades of hard work, is not difficult to understand. (*Credit: People's Palace Museum*)

EUSTACCHIO AND ROSARIA COCOZZA BEHIND THE COUNTER OF THEIR SHOP, HAMILTON, 1920S
In this splendid interior shot, the couple again look enormously proud as they pose in front of their gleaming bottles and large 'sweetie jars'. Italian businesses were always characterised by their high levels of cleanliness and the care taken in presenting a stylish yet homely atmosphere. As we can see, Rosaria is pregnant. After the birth of children, it was common for wives to return to work in the shops leaving their children in the care of young Italian girls, whose first role on arriving in Britain was often as nanny and housemaid. Both Rosaria and her husband had arrived in Scotland in the early 1900s from hamlets in the *comune* of Venafro (Is). (*Credit: A. Di Mambro*)

GIUSEPPE DORÀ, THE BRIG RESTAURANT, ALYTH, PERTHSHIRE, 1921
Born in the *comune* of Borgo Val Di Taro (Pr) in 1899, Giuseppe had first come to London as a boy, with his father, in the early 1900s. They had a roasted chestnut stand near Victoria Station and later opened a provisions shop in Pimlico. As a young man he returned to Italy and later served in the *Alpini* during the First World War. In 1921 he left his village again and came to Alyth to join his elder brother Agostino. The magnificent fish frying machine on which Giuseppe is leaning would have been coal-fired, the fire beneath heating the fat in the vats. It was quite a skill to keep the heat at the correct temperature for frying. From Alyth, Giuseppe moved between Dundee, Arbroath and Aberdeen working for relatives and *paesani* before finally settling in Beith, Ayrshire, in 1933, when he married and set up his own business. This business continues today in the hands of his son Mario. (*Credit: M. Dorà*)

L. FERRARO FRUIT SHOP, ELEPHANT AND CASTLE, LONDON, 1930S
The Ferraro family had been established in Waterloo from around 1865. By around the turn of the twentieth century, L. Ferraro & Sons had become fruiterers, gradually introducing ice-cream. In the 1930s ice-cream was sold from a small part of the shop and from the van in the photograph. The combination of ice-cream and fruit was a common one; over-ripe fruit could be used for fruit ices. By the 1950s, the two shops, 15 and 15A, were separated, with one for fruit and one for ice-cream. The ice-cream parlour, which was operational until 1984 in the hands of Andrew Ferraro, had a 'through window' for service to the street, and wooden tables and chairs inside. (*Credit: K. Sumner*)

ANTONIO AND MADDALENA MANCINI, AYR, 1935
This couple arrived in London from Atina (Fr) in the early 1900s. After a few years they moved
north to Glasgow and eventually settled in Ayr around 1913. They opened their first shop in
King Street. In 1925, Antonio built their second business, The Royal Café, on the New Road out
of Ayr. (*Credit: M. Mancini*)

THE ROYAL CAFÉ, AYR, 1935
Initially this café was a one-storey building, but in 1935 Antonio built living accommodation for
the family, now three sons, on top. When he lost his life in 1940, on the *Arandora Star*, Maddalena
sold the King Street shop and carried on the business at New Road with her eldest son, Michael.
Today, this family business is still prospering under the control of Michael and his son, Philip.
Philip Mancini is the representative for South West Scotland in the Ice Cream Alliance, and is a
key figure in the development of the industry in the 1990s. (*Credit: M. Mancini*)

**SERAFINO AND DORINDA BACCHETTA, PORTH, GLA-
MORGAN, 1930S**

Serafino was born in Gazzo in the *comune* of
Bardi (Pr) in 1899. In 1914, he left his parents to
join two older brothers already in Wales working
for the Rabaiotti family in Newbridge. During
the First World War he and one brother returned
to Italy to do military service. His brother was
killed and in 1920 Serafino returned alone to
Wales, rejoining his other brother. Together they
worked for the Tambini family in Gilfach Goch.
Just before his marriage Serafino was running
one of the Tambini shops for a share of the profits. Dorinda Sidoli, his wife, was also born in
Bardi, at Chiesa Bianca. At 14 she too left home
and had been in domestic service in Milan before
arriving in Wales. The couple had four children.
Two of these, Aldo and Renato, are still in business in Porth today, in the premises below, that
were first bought by Serafino.
(*Credit: A. Bacchetta*)

THE STATION CAFÉ, PORTH, GLAMORGAN, 1930S
Serafino Bacchetta had first come to Porth in 1932 leasing the Station Café from the Rabaiotti
brothers. During the 1930s average weekly takings were around £80 and by 1940 had risen to
£120 a week, with Sunday being the best trading day, taking almost as much as the rest of the
week in that one day. In 1943 when the Rabaiotti lease expired, Serafino took it over, and in
1957, 25 years after moving into the premises, he bought it outright for £200. Later he bought
the premises on either side of the Station Café and today the Bacchetta business consists of a
café, a confectioners, a delicatessen and a restaurant. (*Credit: A. Bacchetta*)

THE RIZZI FAMILY, LONDON, 1920S
Standing at the back are Giovanni and Susanna Rizzi. Giovanni had walked to England in 1876 from Casanova in the *comune* of Bardi (Pr). His three sons seated, are from left to right, Peter, Giuseppe and Antonio. In 1932, the three brothers opened their famous 'Peter & Mario's' restaurant in Soho. When this institution finally closed in 1985, it was the last Italian restaurant in the now exclusively Chinese Gerrard Street. The Rizzi family name, however, remains well known in the catering trade and Florindo (Fred) Rizzi, the son of Peter, is today the proprietor of 'Papagalli's' in Swallow Street, Piccadilly. (*Credit: F. Rizzi*)

THE MARLETTA FAMILY, GREENOCK, C. 1925
One of the major effects of emigration on the Italian family was to divide it and scatter its members, often across the world. When people were forced to leave home, they had to go wherever work and opportunity could be found. Not all members of a family would always be fortunate enough to find work in the same location. But the family is the most important institution in Italian society and its members would fight hard to maintain ties and remain in contact with each other. Here, from this picture of a family group, we can see that the photograph is in fact a 'photomontage' — not all members were present at the same location for the group portrait. The young man at the back, obviously larger than the others, is a cut-out from another photograph which has been super-imposed on to the family group and then re-photographed. Such spiritual efforts at reuniting the family were not uncommon. (*Credit: A. Rossi Chiocconi*)

THE GUARNIERI FAMILY REUNITED AT THEIR FARM IN CELERE CARPANETTO (PC), 1936
Although Emilio and Maria Guarnieri never emigrated, it became necessary for them to send
some of their eight children to London to earn a living. In the mid 1920s, Giuseppina and Gino,
second and third from the left, at 14 and 12 years of age respectively, were sent to work for
distant relatives at their cafés. Faustina (extreme left) and Valentina (extreme right) were also
sent over, but they could not obtain work permits and returned. In 1936, Gino and Giuseppina,
now grown up, returned to visit their parents. The photograph was taken on this occasion. In
1949, Maria, second from the right, arrived in London, where she remains today. In 1975,
Giuseppina returned to Italy while Gino maintains homes in London and Chiavari (Ge), travelling
regularly between the two. Mario (in the middle) and two sisters, Luisa on his left and Netta on
his right, never emigrated. Six of Luisa's seven children, however, emigrated to London in the
1950s and, until her death, she lived six months of the year in Italy and six months in London.
This family story aptly demonstrates how emigration is never a static process. Through family
ties, links are maintained and in every generation there is always an on-going relationship
between 'home' and the new 'home from home'. (*Credit: G. Guarnieri*)

THE MANFREDI FAMILY, BEDONIA (PR), 1920S

After more than 20 years in Leigh, Lancashire, Tioffolo Manfredi is pictured here with his family after returning to their native Setterone in the *comune* of Bedonia (Pr). Around 1900, Tioffolo's brother Davide had walked to England and set up business in Leigh, Tioffolo following later. Between 1900 and 1915, Davide brought over a number of boys from his village to work for him. One of these was Domenico Manfredi who found the going tough and ran away to his uncle, a Federici, in St Helen's. Eventually he was found and brought back, this time to work for Tioffolo at his shop in Duncans Road, Leigh. In 1920, his 'apprenticeship' complete, Domenico bought the business, allowing Tioffolo to return home. Domenico's son, Antonio, continued this business in the original premises in Leigh, until 1990. (*Credit: A. Manfredi*)

THE GRANELLI SISTERS WITH GIOVANNI LONGIN-OTTI, BLACKPOOL, EARLY 1920S

Pictured here, on a day trip, are four of the five Granelli sisters. The girls' father, Louis Granelli, had arrived in Manchester in the late 1880s from Santa Maria del Taro (Pr). Although most of the Italians who reached Manchester in this era originated in the *Ciociaria*, three or four families had come from the Upper Val Taro. Louis sold roasted potatoes and chestnuts around the streets before moving into ice-cream. Ida, in the centre of the back row, is the eldest and married to Giovanni Longinotti, who also came from Santa Maria del Taro. Rosa too, standing on the left, later married a boy from her father's village, also a Granelli, and today her son, Louis Granelli, continues the business started by his grandfather, in the wholesale manufacture of ice-cream, and is one of the largest suppliers to the north of England. (*Credit: L. Granelli*)

YOUNG *FASCIO* MEMBERS, EDINBURGH, 1933

Standing, from left to right: Benny Zaccardelli; Maria Iacovelli; Benny Rossi; seated: sisters Margherita and Filomena D'Agostino. Photographed before setting out for a dance at the *fascio* in Edinburgh, these young people were typical of the British-born second generation in their attitude to fascism. For them it meant identification with the land of their forefathers and, at the same time, an acceptable means of socialisation. Parental approval for involvement in the fascist movement, and the comprehensive set of social activities that this offered, was easily found. Participation kept the younger generation within the Italian fold and ensured the possibility of finding Italian spouses. (*Credit: M. Renucci*)

EX COMBATTENTI, LONDON, 1920S

It was veterans of the First World War such as these men, pictured outside Westminster Abbey, who formed the nucleus around which facism took root in the Italian Communities of Great Britain. Men of the Italian Community who had fought in the war were considered true patriots, especially those with military honours, and were given high status within the newly forming fascist clubs where they became the flag and insignia bearers. (*Credit: La Voce*)

FASCISTI AT WESTMINSTER ABBEY, LONDON, 1920S

London *Fascisti* commanded by Captain Gelmetti saluting outside Westminster Abbey, where they placed a wreath on the grave of the Unknown Soldier. (*Credit: La Voce*)

THE COMMITTEE OF THE *CLUB COOPERATIVO* ASSEMBLE UNDER A PORTRAIT OF BENITO MUSSOLINI, GREEK STREET, SOHO, 1930S

During the 1930s the *Club Cooperativo* was the centre of fascist activity in London until the new *fascio* opened in Charing Cross Road in 1937. Increasingly, the activities of the Italian Community – social, economic and political – came under the influence of fascism and at this centre in Greek Street, the meetings of most of the Community's clubs and associations took place. The offices which organised the teaching of the Italian language to children in the *dopo scuola* were also here. The aim of the fascist movement, outside Italy, was to organise the immigrant Communities and to gather them into a corporate body with a sense of allegiance and patriotism towards Italy. The range of social activity and the sense of dignity which these prestigious clubs gave to the previously unorganised and abandoned Italian Communities were irresistible to the vast majority of Italians. (*Credit: La Voce*)

MEN OF THE ITALIAN COMMUNITY, ABERDEEN, 1925
<u>Front Row</u>, from left to right: Andrea Zanrè; Terroni; Berni; G. Agiustapace; Unknown; Arturo Razzoia; Signorini; Giulianotti; Dick Signorini; Luigi Marcella. <u>Second Row</u>, from left to right: Unknown; J. Carcone; R. Tortolano; P. Ferrari; Giulianotti; Pizzamiglio; Bonici (from Elgin); Joe Giulianotti; Unknown; Unknown. <u>Third Row</u>, from left to right: Eddie Giulianotti; E. Becci; Fred Carcone; Tony Allessandro; Unknown; Luigi Zecca; Joe Berni; Vicci Giulianotti; Vittorio Bicocchi (from Peterhead); Fuccacia; Canon Grant of St Mary's Church. <u>Back Row</u>, from left to right: Tom Crolla; Pat Crolla; Sandy Becci; Meconi; Andrea Zecca; Costante 'Papardella' Zanrè (from Forres); Unknown; Dorà (from Torry); R. Marcella; P. Tortolano. (*Credit: A. Zanrè*)

BENIAMINO GIGLI SINGING WITH THE CHOIR AT ST PETER'S ITALIAN CHURCH, LONDON, 1930s
The most famous Italian opera singer of this era was a frequent visitor to the British Italian Community. He sang not only at the Italian Church but also gave performances at the Charing Cross Road *fascio* and made visits to the *Casa d'Italia* in Glasgow. The Italian Church was also a supporter of the fascist movement in the 1930s and, at the time of the Abyssinian War in 1936, held a special day, the *Giornata delle Fedi*, in which the Italian women of the Colony swapped their gold wedding rings for metal ones, the gold going towards the war effort. (*Credit: E. Asserati*)

THE *CASA D'ITALIA* FOOTBALL TEAM, GLASGOW, LATE 1930s
During the 1930s the *Casa d'Italia* in Glasgow was one of the *fascio* flagships in this country. The main London *fascio* did not open until 1937 and the *Casa d'Italia*, with its entrance of marble pillars and sweeping staircase leading to a grand ballroom, was a club and centre of which the Italians in Glasgow were enormously proud. Although the *Casa* itself had been founded independently in 1935 by a group of local business-men, the *fascio* which had been in existence in Glasgow since 1922, soon took it over. *Fasci* were established throughout the entire country in this era and the Football League which grew up between them was very popular, bringing the men of different Italian Communities into contact with each other – a process which helped in building an overall sense of Community and solidarity. (*Credit: R. Colpi*)

THE LONDON *FASCIO* SUMMER HOUSE, FELIXSTOWE, 1929
A large group of London Italian children have a summer holiday. For over ten years, children of both the Clerkenwell and Soho Italian Colonies were sent to summer camps at the *fascio* summer house in Felixstowe. Such an opportunity, for a fortnight or so at the sea, led to fierce competition for places. Under the direction of Dr Rampagni of the Greek Street *fascio*, these holidays were popular with both children and parents alike. With the *Balilla*, or youth movement, and patriotic singing of *Giovinezza*, the fascist ideology attempted to bring children, as well as their parents, under its influence. (*Credit E. Salvoni*)

ANNUAL PILGRIMAGE AND OUTING TO NORTH WALES, 1927
First organised by the Manchester Italian Society in 1925, this pilgrimage to Pontasaph gathered together Italians from Manchester, Middlesbrough, Wigan, Huddersfield, Warrington, Chester, Liverpool and Sheffield. Normally between 400 and 600 people attended, and from a meeting point at Holywell Junction, they made their way on foot to the sanctuary of Pontasaph. Stations of the Cross were followed by a picnic and the general enjoyment of a day out in the country. Held on 15 August, this event continues to be popular with the Italian Community in the north of England. (*Credit: A. Rea*)

THE ITALIAN CLINIC, PINE STREET, LONDON, 1930S
The clinic was established in the 1930s by the local authority just north of the Clerkenwell Colony. This initiative probably represented one of the first taken by local government to help the Italian 'ethnic minority'. The London Borough of Islington continues this policy of making special provision for the large Italian presence in their area and the FILEF Italian Community Centre is mainly funded in this way. (*Credit: Finsbury Library*)

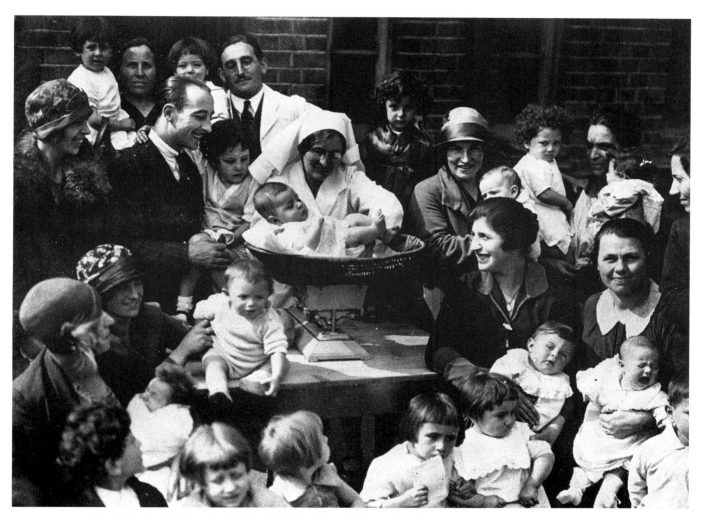

THE ITALIAN CLINIC, MATERNITY CENTRE, PINE STREET, LONDON, 1930S
The photograph shows Italian mothers and children at the clinic of Dr Booth (in the white coat) assisted by Dr Briondi. Italian families at this time were still large, with an average of five or six children. With the establishment of this clinic and the Italian Hospital, medical care of Italians in London was well covered. (*Credit: Finsbury Library*)

FILOMENA D'AGOSTINO WEARING THE *CIOCIARIA* COSTUME, ATINA, 1933
Born in Edinburgh, Filomena married Benny Zaccardelli at the age of 17 and on honeymoon they returned together to Atina (Fr) and Isola Liri (Fr), the villages from which their parents had emigrated. Wearing the local costume was still common in everyday life then and naturally this would give an increased sense of belonging to girls born abroad, as well as helping them learn about and feel proud of their heritage. (*Credit: M. Renucci*)

NORINA ZECCA AT HER FIRST COMMUNION, ABERDEEN, 1933
Born in Aberdeen, Norina's father, like so many of the Aberdeen Italian Community, was from Val Dena in the *comune* Borgo Val di Taro and, although her mother was Scottish, she grew up very much within the Italian Community, making her *prima comunione* at St Mary's and later marrying Tony Zanrè, also of Italian descent. Later in life she returned to studying and as a mature student completed a degree in Italian, going on to teach the language in an Aberdeen Secondary School. (*Credit: N. Zecca Zanrè*)

MARIO RENUCCI, GLASGOW, 1933
Mario, the youngest son of the Renucci family (see top photo on p. 30) was typical of many of the second generation of Scottish Italians at this time who were attending university and obtaining degrees. The first professionals, mainly teachers, lawyers and doctors, began to emerge. After his BSc in mathematics, Mario Renucci in fact became an eminent mathematician at Glasgow University. (*Credit: M. Renucci*)

HOME ON HOLIDAY, VIAREGGIO (LU), 1929
Augusta Marchetti with her son Giorgio, and on the right, Rosa Salteri. Augusta had emigrated from Barga (Lu) to Scotland in 1920 in order to marry. Engaged to a boy who had left their village just after the First World War, her wedding took place in Glasgow. Here with her son, she visits her sister at home in Barga and together they spend a day at the seaside.
(*Credit: P. Marchetti*)

THE *MADONNA DEL ROSARIO* IN PROCESSION, MANCHESTER, 1920

The statue of the *Madonna* was kept at St Michael's Church in George Leigh Street in the Ancoats Italian Colony. Here the Italians gathered before setting out in procession to join the rest of the 'Whit Walk'. In the centre is *Cav.* Domenico Antonelli, President of the Manchester Italian Catholic Society and instigator of the Italian participation in the Manchester 'Whit Walk'. Only men, who carried the statue, and unmarried women were allowed to surround the *Madonna*. Wearing the traditional *Ciociaria* costume was compulsory for girls and women alike in this period. (*Credit: A. Rea*)

THE PROCESSION OF THE *MADONNA DEL CARMINE*, LONDON, 1920S

The large crowd and festival atmosphere is again apparent, the streets filled with Italian (monarchist) flags and flower garlands. The statue seen here, forming part of the procession, is Santa Lucia, carried by the young girls of the Colony. (*Credit: La Voce*)

A GROUP OF SCOTTISH ITALIAN MEN REUNITED IN BORGO VAL DI TARO (PR), 1923
The men in this photograph are cousins who arrived in Britain between 1900 and 1920, reaching Scotland via the London Italian connection. Five years after the First World War, they were prospering and returned home to their village for a holiday. The Manzotti photographic studio was in operation for over forty years and performed a crucial role in documenting the people of, and the emigration from, the Val Taro. People had photographs taken to send to their family abroad. Group portraits were taken before family members emigrated and when individuals returned either permanently or for visits. This photograph was taken to commemorate their first reunion. From left to right: Johnny Dorà from Arbroath; Giuseppe Dorà from Beith; Peter Dorà from Arbroath; and sitting, Joe Berni from Aberdeen. (*Credit: R. Dorà*)

THE SAME GROUP OF MEN AGAIN REUNITED AT BORGO VAL DI TARO, 1953
Each man experienced a different fate in the Second World War, notably Giuseppe Dorà who
was a survivor of the *Arandora Star*. It was several years after the war before they were again
able to return together to their village. However, again in the Manzotti studio, the cousins adopt
the same pose with amusing precision belying the three decades which separate the two portraits
and the momentous events of those 30 years. (*Credit: R. Dorà*)

CHAPTER FIVE

The War and The 1940s

The outbreak of war in 1939 soon led to the end of the period of stability enjoyed by the Italian Community. The events of June 1940 plunged the British Italian Community into the most difficult period of its history and had a devastating effect on many Italians. It began with Mussolini's declaration of war on Britain and the Allies on 10 June 1940, which immediately gave rise to a night of rioting against the Italians resident in Britain. These nationwide anti-Italian riots were particularly severe in Scotland where a very high proportion of Italian shops and cafés were smashed, burned and looted. Large crowds gathered in anti-Italian demonstrations and in Edinburgh, for example, it took several police baton charges to disperse an angry crowd of over 1,000 people.

When we consider not only the length of the Italian presence in this country, and the fact that by 1940 many families had been peacefully settled here for more than a generation, (and also the level of integration and respectability achieved by this time), these events seem astonishing by standards of behaviour in Britain today.

Occurring simultaneously with this rioting was the arrest of the entire Italian male population between the ages of 17 and 60, a direct result of Churchill's now notorious dictum, 'Collar the lot'. As with so many of his sayings the words are not only memorable, but also emotive and provocative. The only justification for this policy was the absence of any prior assessment by the British authorities of the level of risk or threat posed by individual Italians.

Although there were few active anti-fascists amongst the ranks of the Italian Community, equally there were few sufficiently determined fascists likely to pose a security risk to their British homeland. The bulk of the rank and file members of the Italian Community were simply fond and proud of their country of origin — and devastated by the conflict of loyalties forced on them by the war.

The Italian Community was torn apart during the war years. Within a single family, certain members could be fighting in the British Armed Forces, while others were interned on the Isle of Man, in Canada or Australia. Other members may have joined the Aliens Corps, or, most tragic of all, they may have been lost in the sinking of the *Arandora Star*.

In addition, the economic progress achieved particularly in the previous two decades was reversed. Many businesses had to close — there was no one to run them, and in most cases, since everything was rationed, especially milk and sugar for ice-cream, they could not continue anyway. In restricted areas of the country, women and children left unsupported after male internment, were forced to move away and, as a consequence were often split up. It was a period of great stress, wrenching and tearing of the Italian family.

Even today, fifty years after these events, there are many people in the 'old' Italian communities who still find it difficult to talk about the events of this period, and their personal suffering. Some exorcism is needed to bring out these wartime events for all those, young and old, in the Italian Community who might wish to question whether such suffering was either justifiable or necessary.

A final note on the last war. Over 140,000 Italian prisoners of war, most of whom had been captured in Africa, were brought to Britain and held in camps up and down the country. Some of these men died while in captivity. Others, notably those interned on Orkney, made a lasting contribution to the local heritage by constructing buildings and creating works of art during their stay. After the war, many of these men chose to remain in this country and integrated themselves into the ranks of the Italian Community by marrying local British Italian girls, providing a further addition to the Community.

THE *ARANDORA STAR* IN HER PRE-WORLD WAR TWO DAYS AS A LUXURY CRUISING LINER ANCHORED AT VENICE, 1930S

This ship set sail from Liverpool late on 1 July 1940 with 712 Italian men who had been resident in Britain on board, bound for internment, as enemy aliens, in Canada. At 6 a.m. on 2 July 1940 the *Arandora Star* was torpedoed by a German U-Boat and 446 Italian men were drowned. Of the survivors, 200 were shipped from Greenock to be interned in Australia, on board the *Dunera*, and the rest, who were severely injured after their ordeal at sea, were sent first to hospitals on the mainland and then to be interned on the Isle of Man. With such a high loss of life, this is the most tragic event in the history of the Italian Community in Great Britain. (*Credit: U. Marin*)

METROPOLE INTERNMENT CAMP, ISLE OF MAN, 1940S
Hotels, boarding houses, and mansion blocks were commandeered by the War Office and were fenced in with barbed-wire to serve as internment camps. The Italians were housed in the Metropole, Palace, Onchan, Granville and Ramsey camps. Length of imprisonment in the camps depended upon the willingness of the internee to help the British war effort. When released, therefore, the men were not generally allowed to return to their businesses, but were instead allocated jobs in industry, agriculture and other useful sectors. (*Credit: Hulton Picture Library*)

A GROUP OF ITALIANS CLEAR BOMB DAMAGE, LONDON, 1940
By the autumn of 1940, the first of the Isle of Man internees who were willing to help with the British war effort had been released. In London they were often assigned to bomb damage clearance. Both the Soho and Clerkenwell Italian Colonies of London sustained considerable damage during the war. Newport Dwellings, Soho, whose inhabitants were 80 per cent Italian, was hit directly by a mine which dropped steadily and visibly in broad daylight, supported by a parachute. People thought it was an airman and many were killed. (*Credit: Hulton Picture Library*)

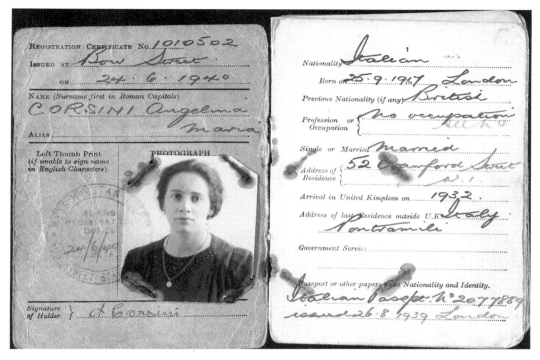

ANGELA CORSINI, A LONDON-BORN ITALIAN GIRL, FROM PONTREMOLI (MS) REGISTERS AS AN ALIEN
SINCE HER HUSBAND IS ITALIAN, 1940
(Even British women who were married to Italians had to register as aliens during the war.)
Angela made four visits to the Isle of Man, where her husband was interned for the duration of
the war. In his absence, she carried on with the family business, a café-restaurant in Barclay
Street, and was helped by Florinda Chiodi. (*Credit: A. Corsini*)

BRUNA CORSINI, LONDON, 1945
Bruna was born in 1940, just before her father
was interned. During the period of the war, in
her first five years of life, she saw her father only
three times during visits with her mother to the
Isle of Man. Interned with Bruna's father was a
member of the Ventura family from Cambus-
lang, Glasgow. Through him, Bruna and her
maternal grandmother were able to move north,
to safety, during the London blitz to live with the
Ventura family in Glasgow. (*Credit: A. Corsini*)

FLORINDA CHIODI, LONDON, 1943
Florinda was a widow when war broke out. She
lost one of her sons on the *Arandora Star* and
another two were interned in Canada until 1945.
She was, therefore, alone during the war and
survived by working for Angela Corsini in her
café-restaurant. (*Credit: A. Corsini*)

A GROUP OF INTERNEES, MAINLY ENGLISH ITALIANS, TATURA, AUSTRALIA, 1943
<u>Back row</u>, left to right: Poggioli; Unknown; Unknown; Cavaciuti; Unknown. <u>Front Row</u>, left to right: G. Scola; Gamberini; G. Boggio; Ferrucio. (*Credit: G. Scola*)

A GROUP OF INTERNEES, MAINLY LONDON ITALIANS, TATURA, AUSTRALIA, 1943
<u>Back Row</u>, left to right: Galbiati; Ugolino Giovine; Giovanni Berni; Pietro Beschizza; Nicola Cua; Francesco Amato. <u>Front Row</u>, left to right: Giovanni Cua; Simonelli; Gino Guarnieri; Vittorio Tolaini. (*Credit: G. Guarnieri*)

A GROUP OF INTERNEES, MAINLY SCOTTISH ITALIANS, TATURA, AUSTRALIA, 1943
<u>Back Row</u>, left to right: G. Tomè; Unknown; Unknown; Sampietro; Costà; Amilcare Cima. <u>Front Row</u>, left to right: Unknown; D. Tomè; Consoli; Randolfo Bertoia; Romolo Chiocconi. (*Credit: A. Pacitti*)

A GROUP OF INTERNEES, MAINLY SCOTTISH ITALIANS, CANADA, 1943
A day after the ill-fated *Arandora Star* set sail, another ship, the SS *Ettrick*, also left Liverpool bound for Canada. Unlike the *Arandora Star*, the *Ettrick* reached its destination. On board, headed for internment on St Helen's Island near Montreal, were 407 Italians. (One man died during the journey). Here and below are some of these men. (*Credit: M. Cattini*)

A GROUP OF INTERNEES, CANADA, 1943
The '*Italia Nord*' football team. There was also an '*Italia Sud*' team. Football was a popular pastime in the camps, especially for the young, and the men organised themselves into teams according to their area of origin in Italy. (*Credit: M. Cattini*)

A GROUP OF INTERNEES, MAINLY ENGLISH ITALIANS, CANADA, 1943
<u>Back Row</u>, left to right: Tino Rossi; Unknown; Luigi Rabaiotti; Monty Cattini; Luigi Gatti; Gino Rabaiotti. <u>Front Row</u>, left to right: Bert Belli; Peter Chiodi; Peter Cattini; Frank Chiodi. (*Credit: M. Cattini*)

THE INTERIOR OF THE 'ITALIAN CHAPEL', LAMBHOLM, ORKNEY, 1944

This chapel was built out of two Nissen huts by the Italian prisoners of war held on Orkney. Captured in Africa, the men had been brought here to work on the fortifications of the Churchill Barrier at Scapa Flow. In 1960 the chapel was restored by Domenico Chiocchetti, the chief architect and designer, who returned to conduct the work. Today the preservation of the chapel is ensured by a local committee, and it is visited annually by large numbers of tourists. Services are held here only in the summer months. (*Credit: A. Lee*)

THE MEN WHO BUILT THE ITALIAN CHAPEL, LAMBHOLM, ORKNEY, 1943

Standing on the extreme left is Chiocchetti, from Moena (Tn), the architect, and in front of the left hand pillar is Palumbo, the smith. The other members of the group, all instrumental in the completion of the chapel, performed various jobs including decoration, carpentry, electric wiring and labouring. These men also transformed their prison camp by laying paths and planting flowers and shrubs, centred on a small *piazza*. (*Credit: J. W. Sinclaire*)

THE 270 COMPANY, ALIENS CORPS, FOOTBALL TEAM, SLOUGH, 1945
The 'A' Company was formed from the internees from the Isle of Man and British-born members of the second generation Italian Community who volunteered to help in the British war effort in a non-active capacity. They were known as the 'Pioneer Corps'. (*Credit: Finsbury Library*)

THE LAST OF THE ISLE OF MAN INTERNEES ARE RELEASED, 1945
Tribunals were held at regular intervals to assess the willingness of the internees to help the British war effort. Many men could not agree to this, even after Italy's capitulation in 1943, and therefore they remained behind barbed-wire until 1945 when most were allowed to return to their businesses. It was a wrenchingly difficult decision for many, especially those who had fought for Italy during the First World War. Group pressure amongst the internees encouraged the individual to remain a 'good Italian', which meant remaining interned with his compatriots. However, often families on the mainland were experiencing enormous hardships and many men felt that their place was at home with their wives and children. Inevitably, among this generation of the Italian Community, factions formed in these difficult times, some of which exist to this day. (*Credit: A. Rea*)

NEWLY-WEDS, ISRAELE CORSINI AND ROSA NEGRI, LONDON, 1946

After the war, as the men returned from internment and the Forces, there was a spate of weddings of the second generation up and down the country. This handsome couple were born in London but came from Braia (Ms) and Carpanetto (Pc). (*Credit: R. Corsini*)

RAZZIANTONIA COCOZZA ON HER WEDDING DAY, HAMILTON, 1944

Razziantonia, born in Hamilton, married a boy from Isernia, the province of origin of her parents. (*Credit: A. Di Mambro*)

DOMENICA DE MARCO ON HER WEDDING DAY, EDINBURGH, 1948
Domenica, like many of the second generation, married out of the Italian Community, and chose
a Scottish husband. (*Credit: D. De Marco Cullen*)

LUIGI, PINA AND TERESA MARIONI IN THE MAN-
ZOTTI STUDIO, BARGO VAL DI TARO (PR), 1946
This portrait was taken just prior to the emigration of these children, with their parents, to
London in 1947. The family are from Grondola
in the *comune* of Pontremoli (Ms) and are waiting
to be 'called for' by their relatives already in
London. The portrait of the children is sent over
in advance. (*Credit Z. Marioni*)

MEN FROM THE HAMLETS OF BRATTO AND BRAIA, PONTREMOLI (MS), LONDON, 1948
The Italian Community begins to re-establish and reorganise itself after the war. In this photo-
graph the thirty or so men who share common origins, reunite in their adopted homeland.
In their midst are the priests from the Italian Church who give a focus for their activity.
(*Credit: P. Beschizza*)

CHAPTER SIX

The 1950s

In the late 1940s and early 1950s an entirely new phase of Italian immigration to Great Britain began: a real 'mass' immigration. Unlike the immigration of the nineteenth and early twentieth centuries, which were maintained by chain migration, the initial stage of immigration to Britain in the 1950s was composed of volunteer workers recruited in bulk.

In the immediate post-war period, during the rapid rebuilding of the British economy, there were certain sectors that needed more labour than could be supplied locally. One inter-governmental initiative taken to solve this problem was an agreement for bulk recruitment schemes between the British Ministry of Labour and the Italian Government. Under these schemes, jobs and work permits were offered to large batches of Italian men and women willing to transfer to this country to work in the various industries where shortages had arisen. The first of these schemes brought over 2,000 young Italian women, 200 at a time, to work in the Lancashire cotton mills. For this scheme, as for others, prior experience was not necessary. Other schemes involved coal miners for Lancashire, Derbyshire and Yorkshire, foundry workers for throughout the Midlands, and tin-plate workers for Swansea.

The most significant of all these groups of people was the one which began to arrive in the summer of 1951, destined for the Bedfordshire brick fields, and continued to flow in from the south of Italy throughout the 1950s and early 1960s. In proportionate terms, one of the largest Italian Communities in Great Britain was thus founded during this period in the town of Bedford, with related Communities in Loughborough, Peterborough, Bletchley and Nottingham. The large southern Italian Community in Bedford today is striking in its size, way of life and range of institutions.

One of the least known groups to arrive in the early 1950s were the coal miners, many of whom were Sicilian. The idea of Italians, and Sicilians at that, working down British coal mines is perhaps one of the most unexpected images of Italian immigration to this country. Between 1950 and 1952, over 1,000 men were drafted into this occupation. A proposal asking for more Italians in 1955 had to be abandoned due to opposition from the National Union of Mineworkers. Substantial numbers, around 700 men, stayed with this occupation and way of life for a decade or more.

There was, however, a continuation of the pre-war type of migration in this decade. Migrants from the old source villages arrived in the traditional destinations of London, Edinburgh, Glasgow and Manchester. Like those who came under the recruitment schemes, it was also necessary for these immigrants to secure a work permit before entry into Britain. Relatives and friends continued to arrange for these as they had done decades ago.

The new immigration substantially changed the overall composition of the British Italian Community at this time. The 'old' areas of settlement and the traditional occupations, mainly in catering, were somewhat overtaken in significance by the 'new' Communities which grew up in locations where often no large numbers of Italians had previously been resident. Not only were these migrants following new occupations, they were from the south of Italy and culturally very different from the descendants of the earlier immigrants who came mainly from northern and central Italy. Furthermore, in the early 1950s, the new migrants came from a vast range of source villages. For all these reasons, the character and structure of the Italian Community, which had up until this time been based on chain migration and strong source and destination connections, changed irreversibly.

TWO HUNDRED *SIGNORINE* ARRIVE AT VICTORIA STATION, LONDON, 1950
Italian women were the first to arrive in England under the 'bulk recruitment schemes' arranged between the British and Italian Governments in the post-war era. The first such scheme approved the entry of 2,000 Italian women between the ages of 18 and 40. These women were destined primarily to work as factory girls on four year contracts in the textile, rubber and ceramics industries of the north of England. By 1950, there were large contingents of these women in Lancashire, Cheshire, Derbyshire and Yorkshire. Indeed, in this early post-war period, Italian female immigration considerably out-numbered Italian male immigration. One result of this was that many of these women married other European Voluntary Workers and stateless persons who had been employed in a similar way. Large numbers of Italian women, especially in Derby, Oldham, Rochdale and Bolton are married to Eastern European, especially Polish, husbands although their children have been brought up entirely within the Italian Community.
(*Credit: Topham Picture Source*)

THE BRICKYARDS, BEDFORD, 1950s
From 1951 to 1961, thousands of Italian men from the south of Italy, particularly from the regions of Campania, Molise and Sicily, were imported by the 'bulk recruitment schemes' to work at the Bedfordshire brickyards. Arriving in batches, they lived initially in hostels set up at the brickfields. Many remained only a short time and returned to Italy. The work was heavy and, for men who had never worked in industrial environments before, adaptation was not always easy. Thousands, however, stayed and established one of the largest Italian Communities in Britain today. In Bedford, the Italians form just under 10 per cent of the town's population. (*Credit: U. Marin*)

HOSTEL ACCOMMODATION, 1950
The main hostels around the brickfields were at Kempston Hardwick, Ampthill, Church Farm, Roundhouse Brogborough, Coronation, Drayton Parslow and Yaxley. Men remained here for varying lengths of time depending on their intended length of stay and their marital status. Single men tended to stay longer before either returning home with their savings or else seeking rented accommodation in the town. Married men, however, were often anxious to bring their wives and families to Britain and, in order to do this, they had to be able to provide accommodation for them. The strain of this demand for rented accommodation in the small town of Bedford soon began to tell. By the late 1950s the town council had banned the brickyards from any more bulk recruitment, although men were still recruited on an individual basis. (*Credit: Hulton Picture Library*)

ITALIAN MINERS, NORTON HILL COLLIERY, SOMERSET, 1951
Between 1951 and 1952 over 1,000 Italians, many of whom were Sicilians from Favara, Canicattì and Canciana (Ag), arrived in England to work at British pits. The vast majority of these were employed at the mines of Lancashire, Derbyshire, Yorkshire and, to a lesser extent, south Wales. Again these work contracts had been set up by inter-governmental agreements, but by 1955, when a new wave of miners was called for, there was much opposition from the National Union of Mineworkers and the schemes came to an end. Many Italians went back to Italy and some of the Sicilians transferred to the Belgian mines. Over 700 from the earlier contingent did stay, however, and transferred to other jobs once their contracts had finished. (*Credit: Topham Picture Source*)

PINO MAESTRI MODELLING PLASTER FIGUREWARE AT HIS WORKS IN HIGHBURY BARN, LONDON, 1953
Although few of the original itinerant *figurinai* settled in London, a tradition of statuette manufacture in factory environments grew up within the Italian Colony unparalleled elsewhere in the country. By the 1930s there were ten statuette factories in London and two of the most famous – Pagliai and Orsi – were in Clerkenwell. Pagliai employed between 60 and 70 men at that time. Pino Maestri, born in London of Lugagnano (Pc) parentage, learned the trade with Pagliai and opened his own business in the 1940s. He was one of the last of this tradition working in London; by the 1960s the Japanese had taken over the production of figurines and statuettes, and there were no Italian firms left in business. (*Credit: Finsbury Library*)

GIOVANNI GALELLI, CHISWICK, LONDON, 1959

In order to staff the growing catering industry after the war, the transference of young workers from Italy continued through family networks and the process of 'chain migration'. At the age of 12, Giovanni was brought over from Fiorenzuola D'Arda (Pc) to work for an uncle in his café-restaurant. He attended school here until he was 14, but worked in all his 'free' time. Here aged 20, Giovanni and his uncle have moved premises to a restaurant in Chiswick. By this time further members of the family have also been brought over to help in the business. In 1974 Giovanni opened his own café-restaurant near Liverpool Street Station, where he and his family worked until its compulsory purchase in 1990. (*Credit: G. Galelli*)

PIETRO PELOSI, PAIGNTON, DEVON, 1950s

The Pelosi family originated in Picinisco (Fr) and arrived in Britain in the 1880s. From initial settlement in London, the family pioneers took two main routes out of the capital. One branch of the family went west, settling in Plymouth, Portsmouth, Paignton and Swansea, and the other branch went north to Scotland, settling mainly in Glasgow and to a lesser extent in Edinburgh. Both Pietro, pictured here, and Gennaro Pelosi had very successful ice-cream businesses on the Torbay Road in Paignton. (*Credit: Ice Cream Alliance*)

THE BESCHIZZA CAFÉ, KNIGHTSBRIDGE, LONDON, 1950S
Cafés and coffee bars flourished across London after the war and more restaurants began to open. Like many small concerns, this was a traditional family business staffed by brothers Pietro, on the right, Danny and Pietro's wife Albina. Pietro and Danny had arrived in London from Bratto, Pontremoli (Ms), with their parents, and Albina is a London-born Italian whose parents came from the nearby hamlet of Braia. They would open at 6 a.m. to catch the early staff at nearby Harrods and would close at 6 p.m. at night. (*Credit P. Beschizza*)

RENZO SERAFINI WITH HIS STAFF, INVERNESS, 1950S
After the war and his internment on the Isle of Man, Renzo returned to Inverness and opened his own shop, which he leased from Biagio Candellini and Patrizio Lunardi for whom he had worked for years before the war. Initially the shop sold fruit and confectionery, but after the war Renzo moved more into an ice-cream and café-type of business. Although now retired from business, he continues, as Italian Consular Correspondent, to do much work for the scattered Italian Community of the north of Scotland. (*Credit R. Serafini*)

THE WEDDING OF LINA PERCONTI AND ALFONSO MORTELLARO, BIVONA (AG), 1952
A traditional Sicilian wedding parade through the village follows the church ceremony. The province of Agrigento became the heartland of Sicilian emigration to England in the late 1950s and throughout the 1960s. During the 1950s, emigration was mainly from the south of Italy, with the movement from Sicily starting later. This young couple are typical of these times, and carried on living in Bivona until 1962 when they went north to Bologna in search of work. By 1965, however, they had arrived in Chertsey, Surrey. A factory production-line job and initial accommodation had been arranged by *paesani* already living in the town. Alfonso now runs an ice-cream van having taken up one of the traditional occupations of the more established Italian Community. (*Credit: L. Mortellaro*)

ITALIANS RETURNING FROM CHURCH ON SUNDAY MORNING, BEDFORD, EARLY 1950S
In this first decade of residence, the Italians attended the local Catholic churches before building their own in 1965. The few women in the picture shows the male dominance of the early Bedford Community. As the men moved out of the brickyard hostels, they shared accommodation in the town, often living several to a room. The previously quiet English county town had never experienced anything quite like this and a spate of letters to the local press talked of 'ear shattering' neighbours. The sort of gregarious parade or *passeggiata* down a quiet Bedford street, pictured here, would most certainly have been a new social phenomenon in the town! (*Credit: Hulton Picture Library*)

LIVING CONDITIONS, BEDFORD, EARLY 1950s
The 'Italian Colony' in Bedford was centred around the Alexandra Road/Midland Road area in the early 1950s. Here large Victorian properties were sub-divided and, by 1958, more than half of the 5,000-odd Italians were living in poor conditions of multi-occupation. Whole families lived in one room and rents charged by unscrupulous landlords were often high. There was a high turnover rate of occupants as families moved often in a constant search for better conditions. (*Credit: Hulton Picture Library*)

NEIGHBOURS, GIBBONS ROAD, BEDFORD, 1958
By the late 1950s, the Bedford Italians began to purchase their own properties, mainly terraced cottages, especially in the Queens Park and the Castle Road areas of the town. By hard work and *sacrifici* the Community began to stabilise and prosper. Also the family ethic began to re-establish itself as the second generation were born. Pictured here in this group, who have come together to celebrate a christening, are some young adults who had come to Bedford in the early 1950s and had quickly established themselves. Luigi and Rosa Giso, the couple standing in the middle, the *compari*, or godparents, to the baby, came from San Sossio Baronia (Av) in 1953. They still live in Bedford today, although two of their four daughters have now returned to Italy to live. (*Credit: R. Giso*)

THE PINI FAMILY, LONDON, 1954

A survivor of the *Arandora Star*, Andrea Pini married Fiorentina Bottali in 1946 on his return to London from internment in Australia. He and his parents owned a café-restaurant in Commercial Street which was in business until 1970. Here, by 1954, his family is established and the children, Luigi, Silvia and Charlie look forward to a bright future as the third generation. (*Credit: F. Pini*)

GIUSEPPE VITTORINI AND FAMILY AT HOME, GLASGOW, 1956

The Italian Community in Glasgow had long since begun to value education as a means of advancement and parents were often keen for their children not to follow them into shop life, but instead to become educated and take up professions. Often, however, children were also expected to work after school and at weekends in the family businesses. Most often, in the city, the house was above the shop and so family life and shop life were in any case interconnected. The back-shop was often the family kitchen and living-room as well as a store-room. Many back-shops were also meeting places, especially for the men of the Community who would visit friends on their half-day off. Games of cards in Italian back-shops were common. (*Credit: Glasgow Herald*)

PRESIDENT GRONCHI OF ITALY AND QUEEN ELIZABETH II, LONDON, 1958
They are proceeding down The Mall towards Buckingham Palace at the beginning of the first state visit of an Italian President to Great Britain after the Second World War. (*Credit: La Voce*)

THE REOPENING AFTER THE SECOND WORLD WAR OF THE *MAZZINI GARIBALDI CLUB*, LONDON, 1951
Founded in 1864 by these two illustrious Italian patriots for the ordinary Italian immigrants, and called the *Società per il Progresso degli Operai Italiani*, this is the oldest and most prestigious of all the Italian clubs and associations in Britain and it is still operating today. During the war, this and other Italian premises such as the Italian Hospital, had been requisitioned by the Custodian of Enemy Property. The reopening of this club held a particular significance for the Italian Community. From left to right: the president of the club, *Cav.Gr.Uff.* Serafino Pini; the Italian Ambassador, Duke Callarati Giotti; the Consul General, Milo Toscani and *Cav.Gran Croce Avv.* Pietro Del Giudice. (*Credit: B. Besagni*)

THE REOPENING AFTER THE SECOND WORLD WAR OF THE ITALIAN, HOSPITAL, LONDON, 1950
Another historic reopening which was important in the process of returning to normal life within the London Italian Community. From left to right: Dr Winsbury White; *Signora* Del Giudice; *Signora* Scelba; the Mother Superior, Anastasia Scoffon; *Signora* Martino; Countess St Elia; *Comm.* Charles Forte. (*Credit: La Voce*)

THE ITALIAN HOSPITAL, QUEENS SQUARE, LONDON, 1959
Founded in 1884 by Giovanbattista Ortelli, a businessman of the London Community, the Italian Hospital was for over a century one of the main institutions of the British Italian Community. From 1958 there was a 'League of Friends' of the hospital which organised charity fund-raising events. When, as a result of falling patient numbers, financial difficulties and on-going management troubles, the hospital was closed down in 1989 by its trustees, Lord Forte and Lord Thorneycroft, there was a sense of great loss in the Italian Community. (*Credit: U. Marin*)

ITALIAN CHRISTMAS DANCE AT THE *CA' D'ORO*, GLASGOW, 1951
When numbers rose as high as 500, which they did for the annual Christmas Dance, the *Casa d'Italia* was not large enough and the event was held at the *Ca' d'Oro* in Union Street. This location was also very popular for the weddings of Glasgow Italians around this time due to the huge first floor function rooms. The Italianate facade of the building, suggested in its name, has been retained although the interior – very much part of the Glasgow Italian social scene for a generation – is now occupied by offices. (*Credit: O. Santoro Marchetti*)

GIOVANNI ROCCHICCIOLI AT THE PIANO IN THE *CASA D'ITALIA*, GLASGOW, 1956
The *Casa* had been closed during the war but was reopened in 1948 and soon became the centre of activity for all generations of the Glasgow Italian Community. In fact the years between 1948 and 1962, were probably the time when it fulfilled the greatest need in the Community for a club, a place to meet, to eat, to drink and generally enjoy an Italian atmosphere. Due to the nature of occupations of the Community, still mostly small shopkeepers, Sunday was always the favourite night of activity. Here we see a group of young people enjoying 'Johnny' Rocchiccioli's playing. From left to right: Esther Docherty, Paula Peritti, Luciana Bertolini. (*Credit: Glasgow Herald*)

MANCHESTER ITALIAN FAMILIES ON A JAUNT, 1950
Members of the Salvatore, Rea, Arcaro and Bagigalupo families on their way to Rhyl in north Wales after the Italian Community's annual pilgrimage to Holywell (see bottom photo on p.81). After the traditional day's outing, driving on to Rhyl became popular after the war as more members of the second generation acquired their own cars. (*Credit: A. Rea*)

ANNUAL *SCAMPAGNATA* OR PICNIC OF THE GLASGOW ITALIANS, ALVA, STIRLINGSHIRE, 1950
Members of the Santoro family, Olga, Arnolfo, Rigo and Emilio share their picnic with Flora Facchini, who is on the right. Organised by the *Casa d'Italia*, this outing was a most popular event throughout the 1950s. It created a relaxed and informal forum for the second and third generations to enjoy each other's company, since young adults were still closely chaperoned during this decade. The *Miss Casa d'Italia* competition was a popular integral part of the *scampagnata*. (*Credit: O. Santoro Marchetti*)

THE INTERIOR, ST PETER'S ITALIAN CHURCH, LONDON, LATE 1950S
Although not many Italians live in Clerkenwell today, St Peter's is still very much the heart of the London Italian Community. Every Sunday, at least 3,000 people visit the church for mass and perhaps a coffee at the adjacent social club. Weddings, christenings, first communions and funerals – the corner stones of life – are conducted here in the Italian way reinforcing the central function of the church in Community life. (*Credit: U. Marin*)

THE LIBRARY, ITALIAN INSTITUTE OF CULTURE, LONDON, 1950s
Opened in the post-war era and part of the attempt to restructure the Italian presence in this country, the Institute is now the main Italian government agency for promoting Italian culture in Britain. The library has over 21,000 books on art, history and literature, and there is a very active programme of cultural events. Since 1987, the Institute has collaborated more with the Italian Community and, through the associations, holds many interesting events in which large numbers of Italians participate. (*Credit: D. Cipriani*)

CHAPTER SEVEN

The 1960s

The bulk recruitment of southern Italians was a short-lived, though intensive, migration concentrated in the early and mid–1950s. From this time and throughout the 1960s, individual firms, however, were able to continue to make requests for workers through the Italian Consular authorities. These requests were filtered back to Italy and the contracts were available through local employment exchanges. Thus, although no large individual batches of workers arrived during this decade, a steady flow and an on-going transferral of workers continued. The migrants were from a myriad of source villages throughout Italy, although again predominantly from the poorer south, and their destinations were principally the Midlands, the East Midlands and the north of England.

Gradually, emigration from Italy worked its way further south and, by the 1960s, large contingents of Sicilians began to arrive in Britain having applied for whatever jobs were available in factories and other unskilled sectors of the economy. While geographical concentrations did build up gradually in certain areas, the overall dispersal of Sicilians throughout the country was remarkably widespread. Of particular note, however, are the many Sicilians who took up market-gardening in Lee Valley, just north of London, and the large numbers who came to fast-growing towns such as Woking and Chertsey, to the south of London. Throughout this decade and the early 1970s, the steady flow of Sicilians arriving in Britain with their families, in search of jobs and accommodation, means that in overall terms, there are more Sicilian-born Italians living in Britain today than there are Italians originating from any other region of the country.

As we have seen in Chapter Six, the arrival of these new groups of migrants sometimes created entirely new Italian Communities. These migrations, however, also brought workers to towns where 'old' Italian Communities already existed. When this occurred, as it did in much of the north of England, especially in the late 1950s and throughout the 1960s, there was little interaction between the two Italian groups. This was particularly true, and remains so today, in areas where the descendants of the 'old' immigration, now in the fourth and even fifth generation, are successful, well-integrated and well-educated Anglo Italians, often originally from the north of Italy, who feel they have little in common with the 'new' immigrants who often have less formal education, come from the south of the country and appear to be less sophisticated.

On the social front, throughout the 1960s there was a growth in the number and the impact of Italian Community institutions. Of particular significance was the foundation of three new Italian ethnic churches: Santa Francesca Cabrini of Bedford, San Giuseppe of Peterborough and the Church of the Holy Redeemer in South London. All established by the Scalabrini Fathers, these churches became the focus for activity in the 'new' Communities especially through the life-cycle events of births, christenings, weddings and funerals. A range of clubs and social events developed around these missions, and made them very much the centre of these Italian Communities in the same way that St Peter's Clerkenwell had been during the last century and indeed still is today. In addition to the churches, several welfare agencies and other Italian semi-governmental bodies appeared in this period, all establishing themselves where the need arose.

By the end of the 1960s, the 'old' Communities had recovered from the worst effects of the Second World War, had re-established their businesses and found anti-Italian xenophobia at last declining on the part of the local populations. The newer migrants were well settled, having purchased homes and raised their families. They were now poised for the major decision of every Italian immigrant – whether to return home or to stay?

ITALIAN NURSERYMEN AMONGST THE CUCUMBER PLANTS, LEE VALLEY, 1969
The valley of the River Lee, a tributary of the Thames, forms one of the best market-garden areas in the country. In the 1960s many Italians came to work in this sector, settling between Enfield and Hoddesdon. The majority came from Mussomeli and Acquaviva Platani (Cl), in Sicily, but there are significant contingents of *Campani* also. The industry supplies London's restaurants with vegetables and its garden centres with house-plants. Stuart Low's Nursery, one of the largest, is owned by Domenico Pascale from Salerno; he employs large numbers of Italian nurserymen and van drivers. (*Credit: La Voce*)

ITALIAN WORKERS, MAINLY WOMEN, AT THE MELTIS FACTORY, BEDFORD, 1960S
The availability of work for women as well as for men in Bedford had ensured the growth and stability of the Community. By 1958, the flow of immigrants to the town was mainly female, as wives joined husbands, and families were reunited. The biggest single employer of women in Bedford in the late 1950s and throughout the 1960s was the Meltis factory, where they formed a hard-working and reliable workforce. (*Credit: U. Marin*)

FRANCESCO PIZZO, BARBER, PETERBOROUGH, 1969
From a tradition of wig-making during the nineteenth century, hair 'dressing', cutting and styling has always been a popular occupation, particularly amongst young Italians who see it as being linked to style, creativity and design. This particular skinhead, does not, however, have much hair left to style! (*Credit: La Voce*)

FRANCO GUERRICO, CARPENTER, 1960s
There were a number of skilled traditions in the 'new' Italian Communities of the 1950s and 1960s, skills which the migrants had brought with them from Italy. Although many started with the four year contracts in unskilled jobs, they were soon able to set up their own businesses with their trades, such as carpentry, plumbing, electrical work and upholstery. Being a motor mechanic also became very popular as an occupation in the second generation of British-born Italians in the late 1960s and early 1970s. (*Credit: La Voce*)

LORENZO PICCHIONI, LONDON, 1967
Lorenzo Picchioni came to London from Stipes (Ri) in 1961 and worked his way up through the catering ranks in the time-worn way. By 1967, in partnership with Matteo Pocicane, he had become a *padrone* in his own restaurant, the Bella Vista. (*Credit: La Voce*)

SILVINO TROMPETTO MBE, *MAÎTRE CHEF DES CUISINES*, **THE SAVOY HOTEL, LONDON, 1969**
By the late 1960s Trompetto was the best-known Italian chef in London, having reached the absolute pinnacle of his profession, with over 100 cooks, 15 pastry chefs and 7 bakers under him at the Savoy. Trompetto came from Ivrea (To) and followed a long line of migrants from the region of Piemonte into the London catering industry. (*Credit: La Voce*)

AN ACCORDION SHOP, LONDON, 1960s

Accordion music has always been popular in the Italian Community. The Binelli brothers of Clerkenwell are very well-known and play not only in the Community but also at celebrated West End restaurants. There were several accordion shops in Charing Cross Road at one time, but only Macari's, the general musical instrument shop, still exists today. (*Credit: Roma Studios*)

THE MARENGHI FAMILY, LONDON, 1966

Luigi Marenghi, on the right, was born in Bardi (Pr) and emigrated to England in 1920 having served as a *bersagliere* in the First World War. His wife, Carolina Zubielna, was born in London of an old London Italian family. During the Second World War they returned to Italy, but in 1947 they came back to London again and set up their first business, a little café in Camden Road. By 1966 they had two cafés and this delicatessen shop. The whole family, four children and parents, were involved in this truly 'family business'. (*Credit: La Voce*)

THE WEDDING OF SANTINA ROMA, BEDFORD 1960S
The first members of the second generation, usually the ones who were born in Italy prior to their parents' emigration, began to marry in the 1960s. In the Italian Communities of Bedfordshire, Northamptonshire, Cambridgeshire and Hertfordshire, there was by this time an enormous pool of eligible partners to choose from. There are almost seventy people in this photograph emphasising the importance, even at this early stage, of the wedding in Community life. It is, after all, through marriage that the family is perpetuated. To honour the family's name the parents are expected to 'do their best' for a wedding and over the next two decades the scale of these events grew, reflecting the increasing economic prosperity of the Community. (*Credit: G. Bavaro*)

A CHRISTENING, BEDFORD, 1962
Over the 1950s decade this large extended family – Bavaro and Manganiello – emigrated to Bedford and Peterborough from the village of Pratola Serra (Av), finding work in the brickyards and at the Meltis factory. The second generation already spans more than a decade in years, from Antonio sitting at the front on the left, who was born in Italy and who is now ten, to the newly-born baby in his mother's arms. After weddings, christenings are the main family celebration in the Community. The couple selected to be godparents, the *compari*, are very important and hold a high status within the family and are almost as close as blood ties. (*Credit: G. Bavaro*)

PROCESSION OF CORPUS CHRISTI, BEDFORD, 1968
Santa Francesca Cabrini, the Italian Church of Bedford, was founded by the Scalabrini Fathers in 1965. So different are the traditions, in cultural terms, of southern Italian Catholics that it was vital for them to have their own church. This was the first Italian parish church founded in Britain after St Peter's Italian Church in London in 1864. Santa Francesca instantly became the heart of all activity within the Bedford Italian Community. The priests acted as social workers, founded a nursery and a youth club, and housed the first Italian welfare agency. The procession of Corpus Christi shown here, organised in conjunction with other local Catholic parishes, was replaced by a traditional procession of patron saints and a *festa* in the 1970s. (*Credit: M. Dalla Costa*)

THE CHURCH OF THE HOLY REDEEMER, BRIXTON, LONDON, 1969
Since the 1930s there had been an Italian chaplain attached to St George's Cathedral, Southwark, to minister to the Italian Community south of the River Thames. The Scalabrini Fathers identified the need for a second Italian parish in London and this church and centre was founded on Brixton Road in 1968. In addition to the church, which was modernised in 1979, the centre offers Italians a range of facilities and is the meeting-place for a number of clubs and associations, notably the *Club Italia*, the *Club delle Donne* and the *Alpini* Choir. The British Italian fortnightly newspapers *La Voce degli Italiani in Gran Bretagna* is published from here and there is also a nursery and a students' hostel. (*Credit: La Voce*)

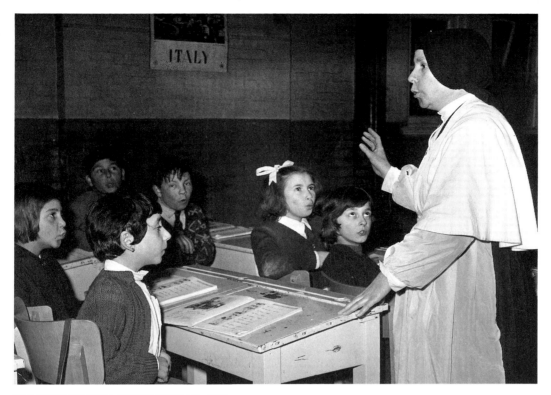

LEARNING ITALIAN, PETERBOROUGH, 1969
Sister Margherita teaches Italian to the British-born second generation. Such classes, still held all over the country, are known as the *doposcuola* because the lessons take place either after school or on a Saturday morning. In the 1960s and 1970s, in the newly-formed southern Italian Communites, many children suffered considerable language problems. When they went to school at five, they spoke only the local dialect of their parents. They had to learn English quickly, and often this was further complicated, since at the *doposcuola*, children were taught the standard Italian language and were therefore placed in a trilingual situation. (*Credit: La Voce*)

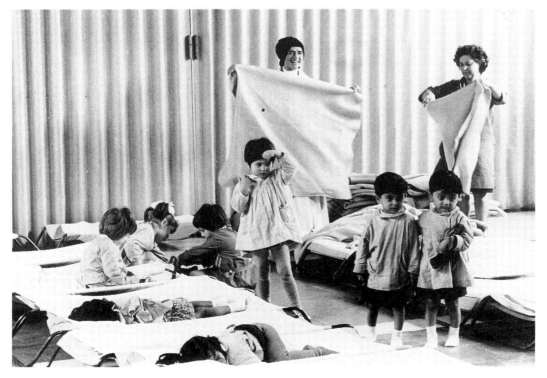

THE AFTERNOON *SIESTA* AT THE NURSERY, BEDFORD, LATE 1960S
Founded in 1961 and under the direction of the working sisters of the House of Nazareth, the nursery in Bedford fulfilled a much needed role in the Community, especially in the 1960s, allowing Italian women to go out to work. Today it continues and cares for many third generation Bedford Italians. (*Credit: La Voce*)

FIRST COMMUNION, ST PETER'S ITALIAN CHURCH, LONDON, 1960S

The First Communion of Catholic children is the most important event in binding children to the Church. It is at this point that they truly become members, being considered sufficiently spiritually conscious to undertake such a step. The *prima comunione* is especially important in another sense too, for children of the Italian Community. Often at non-Catholic schools, particularly in England, this coming together in the Italian-Catholic environment is culturally as well as spiritually educational. The period of religious instruction puts them in touch with their Italian peers and they begin to learn about the Italian institutional environment. (*Credit: A. Ferrari*)

FIRST COMMUNION, SAN GIUSEPPE, PETERBOROUGH, 1968

Where children do attend Catholic schools, there has often been some difficulty in organising their participation in the purely Italian Communion groups. In Peterborough, where the Italians have their own church, this has not been so, and every year between 40 and 60 Italian children make their *prima comunione* together in the Italian way at San Giuseppe. (*Credit: La Voce*)

THE YOUTH CLUB, BEDFORD, 1960s
By the 1960s, the difficulty of imposing southern Italian village traditions on teenagers brought up in urban Britain became a problem for the first generation immigrants. For boys, like the ones pictured here, peer groups developed and their solidarity often challenged the authority of the family, introducing for the first time the generation gap. Girls had less freedom and even the youth club, founded by the priests at the Italian Church, was not considered a suitable social venue for them. Very few of the second generation in Bedford, however, became rebels and most, especially after marriage, settled down to a life style quite similar to that of their parents. (*Credit: La Voce*)

A GROUP OF ITALIAN CHILDREN, CARDINAL BOURNE SCHOOL, LEE VALLEY, 1968
As pupils became older, taking part in the *dopo scuola* classes was also seen as a means of socialisation, since they had their parental approval for attendance. This was especially true for girls who had a very limited range of social activities open to them. Sitting, from left to right: Franco Castiglione; Antonietta De Piano; Maria De Luca; Giuseppina De Feo; Antonio Filarmonico. Standing, from left to right: Nicola Castiglione; Antonio Cuffaro; Lorenzo Rodia; Fiore Agnese. (*Credit: La Voce*)

'GIORGIO AND MARCO'S MEN', WOLVERHAMPTON, 1966
Started by the brothers Giorgio and Marco Uccellini, this group became one of the most famous Italian pop bands in the country with their disc 'Run Run'. Forming pop groups has, since the 1960s, been an extremely popular activity amongst the second generation. The opportunity for recognition within the Community and the chance to present a *bella figura* is irresistible to the Italian who believes he or she possesses some musical talent. The best of the bands, which in London have become small orchestras, are very popular and provide entertainment at large weddings and dinner dances. (*Credit: J. Lines*)

DINNER DANCE, BRISTOL, 1964

Over 700 Italians from the counties of Avon, Wiltshire, Somerset, Gloucester and Devon, gather for their sixth annual dinner dance and *festa*. The Italian Communities of these areas were established in the post-war era; the two main concentrations of Italians are in the towns of Bristol and Swindon. The Swindon Community is composed of a large contingent of *Calabresi*, and in Bristol there are many Sicilians. They are mostly employed in the many light industrial factories of the area. (*Credit: La Voce*)

***MISS EMIGRANTE* COMPETITION, FINSBURY TOWN HALL, LONDON, 1964**

Family dinner dances had become a popular night out in the 'old' Italian Communities in the 1930s but it was not until the 1960s, with the new wave of immigration, that these events became a regular feature of Community life. By this time, the immigrants of the 1950s had achieved some degree of economic prosperity and were increasingly able to afford to organise such evenings. The *Miss Emigrante* competitions were popular throughout the 1960s and 1970s and gave teenage girls some status within the Community for the first time. (*Credit: La Voce*)

THE *ARANDORA STAR* MONUMENT, ST PETER'S ITALIAN CHURCH, LONDON, 1960

A bronze plaque by Mancini was mounted on the outside wall of St Peter's, above the First World War Memorial. It symbolises a lifeboat and commemorates the 446 Italians who lost their lives on the *Arandora Star* during the Second World War. A committee composed of some of the survivors and members of the *Mazzini Garibaldi Club* were responsible for this commemorative initiative. (*Credit: La Voce*)

THE *ARANDORA STAR* PLAQUE, 1960

The inscription reads 'To the Memory which lives on in the Hearts of the Relatives, the Survivors and the Italian Community.' (*Credit: La Voce*)

SURVIVORS AND FAMILIES OF THE VICTIMS OF THE *ARANDORA STAR*, LONDON, 1960

Gathered together at this historic ceremony at the Italian Church were survivors: Dino Accini; Luigi Beschizza; D. Borzoni; C. Casali; Ferrari; Gino Guarnieri; Andrea Pini; Serafino Pini. The presence of the Italian authorities indicated the willingness of the Italian state to recognise this war time tragedy in some official way. From a small gathering of around seventy people in 1960, the annual commemoration of the *Arandora Star* at St Peter's now attracts several hundred people and keeps the tragedy and its surrounding circumstances very much a living memory in the hearts of the 'old' Italian Community. (*Credit: Londra Sera*)

CUP FINAL, ANGLO ITALIAN FOOTBALL LEAGUE, LATE 1960S
Founded in 1965 and still highly successful within the Italian Community, the League now, in 1991, consists of 20 teams from all over the country with more than 600 people involved. The Italian authorities are also involved and the main trophy for which teams compete is the *Coppa Console Generale*, seen on the table with the other smaller 'Sportsman's Trophies' awarded to all players in the Cup Final. (*Credit: R. Nante*)

ANGLO ITALIAN FOOTBALL LEAGUE, FIRST DIVISION TEAM 'PARTENOPEI' OF BEDFORD, 1969
The sponsorship of teams gives present-day *padroni* in the Italian Community a means of personal promotion in an acceptable and Community-enhancing way. Teams often take the names of their businesses or, alternatively, the name of the association or club which funds and organises them. Standing, from left to right: *Cav.* G. Ciampa; M. Ruta; E. Cunto; G. Torchia; F. Avenia; M. Picciano; G. Riccio; M. Cunto. Kneeling, from left to right: G. Megale; M. Dolente; A. Marinaro; F. Bulzis; F. Megale. (*Credit: R. Nante*)

SPAGHETTI-EATING COMPETITION, BEDFORD, 1965
When the Italian Church, Santa Francesca, was built in Bedford the priests immediately organised a *festa* along the traditional village lines in the large garden behind the church. It was this sort of event, which, from the late 1960s onwards, gave a focus to the Italian Community in Bedford. (*Credit: U. Marin*)

PRESIDENT SARAGAT OF ITALY, ALBERT HALL, LONDON, 1969
After his state visit to Great Britain, President Saragat met with the Italian Communities of England and Scotland. Here at the Albert Hall, packed to capacity with Italians from London and the south east, he expounds on the value of keeping alive Italian language and culture in the new generations of the Community. President Saragat also visited Glasgow and the Scottish Italian Community at the *Casa d'Italia* which he 'officially' reopened after its closure during the Second World War. (*Credit: La Voce*)

THE CONSUL GENERAL, COUNT PAOLO VALFRÈ, GIVING AN INTERVIEW, LONDON, 1965
As part of his Christmas message, broadcast on the BBC Italian Service, Count Valfrè said to Sergio Gazzarrini (the interviewer) that 'Italian workers who have emigrated to Great Britain are very well integrated; they are looking to the future with confidence and peace of mind.' The same could be said today. (*Credit: BBC*)

THE PROCESSION OF THE *MADONNA DEL CARMINE*, LONDON, 1969
The happy atmosphere of this crowd scene is captured as the *Madonna* returns to St Peter's having visited her territory. The elaborate box upon which the *Madonna* is mounted, making the statue more visible to the crowd, requires eight bearers for strength and balance. (*Credit: A. Ferrari*)

CHAPTER EIGHT

The 1970s

The 1970s saw very little new immigration to Britain from Italy, and in fact for the first time the number of Italians returning home to Italy exceeded the number coming to Great Britain. Many of the migrants of the 1950s and 1960s fulfilled their intention of staying only a certain time, working hard and returning home with their savings.

There was, however, a new and temporary flow from Italy — that of students: young people who came here on working holidays and to learn English. With Britain's entry into the European Community, this became possible and even fashionable. These migrants came for short periods, had no intention of staying and did not add either numerically or socially to the Italian Community as such, except perhaps in London where their presence was greatest.

During the 1970s, life in the Italian Community continued much as it had in the 1960s. There was a growing prosperity and a growing integration. In the 'old' Communities, many of the traditional occupations continued. The link with catering was consolidated, especially in London. Chain migration recruits of the 1950s and 1960s opened their own sandwich bars, restaurant-cafés, *trattorie* and restaurants, all the while gaining a new sophistication due to improved communication and contact with Italy. Many long established businesses dating from the 1920s and before, however, finally folded in this decade, the descendants of the owning families — by now in the fourth generation — having followed a different path. The most outstanding empire to emerge on the international stage was that of the Forte family, which had begun, in the same way as every Italian business in the country, with a single café in Alloa in Scotland.

The 'old' Communities, in many cases, were beginning to fade as third and fourth generation people opted out of the Italian fold, preferring instead to merge into the local population. This took place naturally through marriage and occupational choices and happened rapidly in areas where no real Italian Community existed. However, as is often the way with Italian Communities, many people in the third generation all across the country took an interest in their past, their roots and heritage. Often such awareness led to a cultural leap which, through the study of Italian language, art and culture at university, has taken these individuals to a broader appreciation of Italy than their forefathers, most of whom, as we have seen, came from simple origins.

In the 'new' Communities also, prosperity and integration were the order of the day, albeit in different ways and to a lesser extent. The Family was the all important unit upon which the southern Italian Communities were based. Most immigrants of the 1950s had purchased their own homes in the 1960s and, by the 1970s, the beautifully kept little terraced house of the Italian family could always be picked out in a street of any English town.

These Italians continued to work long hours but, even on labourers' and factory-workers' wages, were able to save enough in order to give their sons and daughters the wedding that their tradition requires. Where numbers have been sufficiently large such as in Bedford, Peterborough and Nottingham as well as in the south east as a whole, few marriages outside the Italian Community have occurred. In these new Communities the members of the second generation who were in the main educated in Britain, tended to move into skilled occupations when they left school. Few progressed to university and polytechnics for further education, but many hope their own children will do so.

The Italian churches remained a social as well as a spiritual focus for the Italian Communities and these, in conjunction with the well organised structure of institutions, clubs, and, increasingly, associations, ensured the survival of the Italian Community as a collective entity.

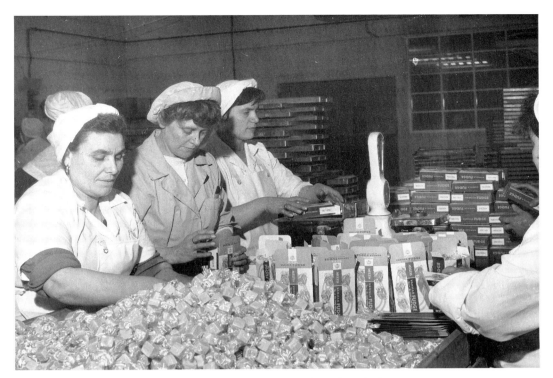

ITALIAN WOMEN WORKING AT THE TOBLER MELTIS FACTORY, BEDFORD, 1975

Working together for many years in the factory environment with compatriots often meant there was little easy opportunity to learn English. Many of these women have now retired after thirty years of service with '*O Meltis*' and still speak very little English. Amongst the first generation in Bedford, in fact, a curious new dialect has emerged which is a combination of village dialects and English. Where no word existed in the Italian dialect they would incorporate English words, but change them slightly in the process. The resultant language can baffle the uninitiated. (*Credit: N. Verby*)

MAKING *LASAGNE*, BEDFORD, 1970s

By this stage in the development of the Italian Community in Bedford, a number of enterprising Italian women had set themselves up in small businesses to cater for the weddings which take place every Saturday of the year during the summer months. There are normally between 200 and 500 guests at these events who expect to be presented with a lavish four-course meal. Families spend a large proportion of their savings on the wedding feast and the other necessary trappings, (for example, *bomboniere*) and a considerable cottage industry has grown to supply these needs. The women pictured here are typical of the small firms which cater for weddings and dinner dances in Bedford and the surrounding Italian Communities. (*Credit: K. S. Studio*)

JACK COIA, ARCHITECT, GLENDARUEL, LATE 1970s

The son of immigrants from Filignano (Is), Giacomo Coia was born in 1898, the eldest of nine children, in Wolverhampton. When Jack was one year old his father bought a barrel organ and, putting his child in a basket on the organ, he and his wife worked their way to Glasgow, grinding their way north. On arrival in Glasgow, they opened a café near Parkhead Cross. Jack studied at St Aloysius School and later at Glasgow School of Architecture. By 1927 he had become a partner in a firm of architects. One of his first works was an extension to the famous *Ca' d'Oro* building in Union Street which, as its name suggests, resembles the building in Venice. In 1931 he received his first commission from the Catholic Church in Scotland. Thus began his numerous and well loved contributions to church architecture, for which he is best remembered. Although born in this country, the basic influence on his work was Italian and it was a dedication to art which moved and directed his life as an architect. (*Credit: W. K. Rogerson*)

FIAT UK LTD, DOVER, LATE 1970s

The managing director of Fiat UK Ltd, *Dott*. G. Boella, the Mayor of Dover, and *Dott*. Stefinlongo, the manager of these new Fiat premises at Dover, inspect the car preparation line. The new six acre site is to be used for preparation of imported cars and as a central stores distribution depot for Britain. Throughout the 1970s and 1980s, Fiat cars grew in popularity in this country and many of the dealerships are in Italian hands, with Carmine Leo now being the largest dealer in London. (*Credit: R. Warner*)

GINO NARDUZZO, MOSAIC WORKER, LONDON, 1975
Carrying on with one of the oldest and most highly skilled of the Italian crafts, Gino, whose father came from Fanna (Pn), Friuli, conducts a delicate restoration operation on an ancient Roman mosaic. (*Credit: U. Marin*)

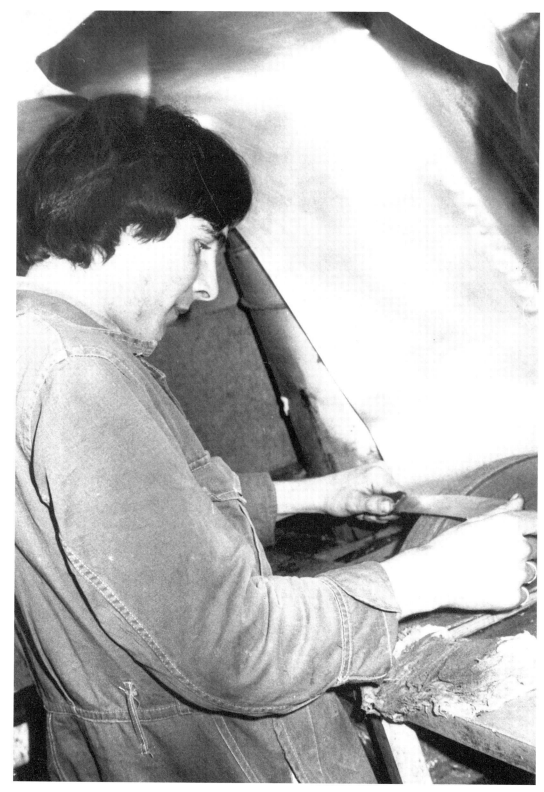

A KNIFE GRINDER, OR *ARROTINO*, LONDON, 1970S
Carrying on with a traditional occupation of the London Italian Community and supplying a most necessary service to London's restaurants, cafés and sandwich bars, the *arrotini* still have something of a monopoly in this field and they continue to recruit in the traditional way from family and *paesani* first. (*Credit: A. Collini*)

THE BERTORELLI BUS, LONDON, 1975
One of the old London Italian families, four Bertorelli brothers emigrated from Bergasi in the *comune* of Bardi (Pr) around the turn of the century. Two went to America and two came to London. Their first catering venture, a pie and mash shop, was set up in 1908, but by 1913 the famous Bertorelli Restaurant in Charlotte Street had been established. During the First World War the four brothers returned to Italy to do military service, and after the war all four came back to London. The ice-cream side of the family business, started by Leo Bertorelli in 1947, and famous for their fabulous ice-cream sculpture, was sold in the 1960s to J. Lyons, who kept the well-known name. The restaurant in Charlotte Street, and three others, closed in 1984, but the tradition continues in the hands of Adrian Bertorelli of the third generation, at his Covent Garden restaurant. His grandfather, Giuseppe, is still alive and, at 98, one of the oldest men in the Italian Community. (*Credit: A. Bertorelli*)

LEONI'S QUO VADIS, DEAN STREET, SOHO, 1970S
One of the oldest Italian restaurants in Soho and still very popular, Quo Vadis was opened in 1926 by Peppino Leoni from Cannero (No) on Lake Maggiore. Although the Leoni family sold the restaurant in the mid-1970s and it is now owned by a non-Italian partnership, the management is Italian and most of the staff have been there for over thirty years. The chef, Vincenzo Sacconi, is particularly well known and loved. Leoni's is one of the last of the grand old restaurants of Soho. (*Credit: La Voce*)

ASSISTENZA VIAGGIATORI, VICTORIA STATION, LONDON, 1970s

Throughout the 1950s and 1960s, the Italian immigrants coming to Britain had arrived by train at Victoria Station and were processed at Platform 8 by Elizabetta Bof, who was awarded the *Cavaliera* by the Italian government for her work with the immigrants. During this time the sign at the station had been *Assistenza Immigranti*. By the 1970s the period of Italian 'immigration' was over and those who arrived were mainly young people — *viaggiatori*, or travellers — who came for short stays to work and to learn English. The sign at the platform changed accordingly, indicating the end of an era. (*Credit: La Voce*)

FRITH STREET, SOHO, LATE 1970s

The Italian Community of Soho had dispersed to the suburbs of London after the war. Remnants of the Italian business community, however, survived until the 1970s, when most finally closed down due to high lease renewal premiums and the growing sleaziness of the area. Several long-established family businesses including Bifulco and Parmigiani, the provisions stores, and Del Monico, the wine merchants, closed in this decade. By the late 1970s, the last concentrated presence of the Italian business connection in Soho was Bianchi's, Bar Italia, Nino's Hair Salon and Angelucci the coffee specialist, in a row, in Frith Street. Today, Bianchi's has closed down, but the other three still remain. (*Credit: La Voce*)

THE *BEFANA* PARTY, *CASA D'ITALIA*, GLASGOW, 1973

More than 160 children of Italian descent aged between 4 and 12 years gather for this annual party and are entertained by two clowns in the best *Grimaldi* tradition. (Grimaldi, known as the 'father of all clowns', was the son of Italian immigrants, born in London in the 1820s. His memory is still an inspiration to clowns today, who hold a mass annually to commemorate him). The *Befana* is 6 January, the feast of the Epiphany, and the giving of presents by the 'good witch' at this time, in the tradition of the three Kings, is more common in Italy than on 25 December. The *Befana* parties have always been a great favourite with Italian children in this country since it seems to them that Father Christmas comes twice. (*Credit: La Voce*)

CHILDREN OF THE ITALIAN LANGUAGE *DOPOSCUOLA* CLASSES, BATTERSEA, LONDON, 1972

These classes are organised jointly by the Italian Consulate Education Department, the Italian parent-teacher committees called FASFA and the Co.As.It., a voluntary assistance body, partly funded by the Consulate and partly by its own fund-raising efforts. The mother tongue language teaching is important in keeping alive not only the language, but also the culture in the second and third generation of British-born Italians. (*Credit: La Voce*)

TERESA BUONAURO, BEARING THE BANNER AT THE 'MARCH FOR ALDO MORO', DERBY, 1978
Organised by Pino Buglione and the Association of Italian Emigrant Families, ANFE, this march
by several hundred local Italians through the main streets of Derby displayed an awareness of,
and involvement in, Italian politics. When Aldo Moro, the Christian Democratic Prime Minister,
was assassinated by the Red Brigades, British Italians were outraged; this march indicated
solidarity with the crisis at home. (*Credit: P. Buglione*)

FESTA DEI NONNI, SCALABRINI CENTRE, LONDON, 1979
From left to right: *Signora* Varesio; *Signor* Corradi; *Signora* Birri. As the Italian Community reaches
maturity and its age structure mirrors the population at large, the number of old people has
increased. There are now two associations for old people, the 'Movement of Old Italians in
England' (MAIE) and the 'Association of Italian Emigrant Pensioners; (APIE) in London. In
addition, in 1986, the first Italian old peoples' home, *Villa Scalabrini*, was opened at Shenley in
Hertfordshire to care for ageing members of the Community. There are presently 40 old people
living there. *Villa Scalabrini* is supported by the Italian Community and, as a registered charity
and through an active programme of events, it is able to provide this valuable service.
(*Credit: A. Vico*)

ARANDORA STAR PLAQUE, GLASGOW, 1975
The men who lost their lives on the *Arandora Star* were also commemorated in Scotland by a plaque which reads *Non vi scorderemo mai* — We will never forget you. The mosaic, by the Scottish artist Selby, was housed in the *Casa d'Italia* until its closure in 1989, and represents the explosion created by the torpedo that struck the boiler room of the *Arandora Star*, causing the ship to sink within thirty minutes. (*Credit: R. Serafini*)

BROOKWOOD MILITARY CEMETERY, SUSSEX, 1975
Over a hundred of the 140,000 Italian prisoners of war who were brought to this country during the Second World War died while prisoners in Britain and were buried at this cemetery. In November each year, a remembrance mass is held here for them, and for the men who lost their lives on the *Arandora Star*, by the military, consular and religious authorities. This ceremony is attended by several hundred members of the Italian Community from the south east. (*Credit: La Voce*)

ITALIANS FROM YORKSHIRE ON AN OUTING TO THE LAKE DISTRICT, 1972
This trip was organised by the Italian Club of Bradford, a town with an Italian Community of around 1,500 people from all regions of Italy. The 'old' Community was supplemented by considerable post-war immigration in the 1950s and 1960s. During the 1970s, bus trips and outings were popular. In more recent years, as affluence has grown, such organised trips have gone further afield with much foreign travel. Organised through the clubs and associations, visiting regions of origin in Italy has become popular too. (*Credit: La Voce*)

ITALIANS FROM LONDON ON AN OUTING TO MARGATE, 1970
Scalabrini missionary priest, *Padre* Silvano Bertapelle, now based in Woking, where he is also Consular Correspondent, leads a party of London Italians on this outing to Margate. Before arriving in England in 1968, *Padre* Silvano had been ministering to the Italian Communities in Australia for 15 years. (*Credit: S. Bertapelle*)

SCAMPAGNATA, OR PICNIC, OF THE LONDON
ITALIAN COMMUNITY, NEAR SUTTON, 1975
Organised by the *Mazzini Garibaldi Club,* the tradition of the annual outing to the country is still
maintained and is growing in popularity rather
than declining. Here, over 2,500 London Italians
gathered for their day together in the country.
A *Miss Scampagnata* competition continues to
be a popular feature of the day's events.
(*Credit: La Voce*)

A GROUP OF HUNTERS, CAMBRIDGESHIRE, 1972
Shooting is very popular amongst the Italian Community, especially with people from the
mountain valleys of Parma and Piacenza. The group pictured here live in London and come
originally from Monastero Val D'Arda (Pc). The main hunting fraternity within the Community
is the *Associazione Cacciatori* which has several hundred members and meets throughout the
winter in various shooting locations in the home counties. (*Credit: La Voce*)

NEWLY DECORATED *CAVALIERI*, ITALIAN EMBASSY, LONDON, 1979
Honours are conferred by the Italian Government upon those members of the British Italian Community who have in some way contributed to Community life, by enhancing its solidarity, cultural and general recreational activity. These awards, which bestow enormous prestige on the individuals who receive them, are highly coveted, and are awarded annually. From left to right: *Cav*. Oscar Gallaon; *Cav*. Vincenzo Cimatti; *Cav*. Romano Conti; His Excellency Ambassador Ducci; *Cav*. Bruno Besagni; *Cav.Uff*. Bruno Roncarati; *Cav.Uff*. Vincenzo Poggi. (*Credit: B. Besagni*)

AGM OF THE ITALIAN CHAMBER OF COMMERCE, LONDON, 1978
The out-going president, Lord (then Sir Charles) Forte, receives a plaque in honour of his services from the new president *Cav.Gr.Uff*. Massimo Cohen. From its prestigious offices in Regent Street, the Chamber is very active in promoting business links between Italy and Britain, and organises a number of conferences, dinners and exhibitions every year with interesting themes and impressive guest speakers. An exclusive inner circle, the *Club di Londra*, is composed of about 100 men — the top Italian businessmen, bankers and diplomats in London today. (*Credit: J. S. Markiewicz*)

THE VILLANI SISTERS, ENFIELD, 1975
The sisters were popular young entertainers in the local Italian Community of Enfield in the 1970s, often playing at Italian social evenings. (*Credit: La Voce*)

LENA ZAVARONI, 1978
After her success on *Opportunity Knocks*, Lena Zavaroni became well known in this country for her lively singing. A third generation Scots Italian, her paternal grandfather came from the Val di Vara in the province of La Spezia, and, like so many of his *paesani*, settled on the Clyde Coast and Estuary, in Rothesay. (*Credit: D. Hoffmann*)

THE ARTIST, FRANCO BERTAGNIN, WITH HIS FATHER, LONDON, 1970
From his studio in Kensington, Bertagnin became increasingly well known in the 1970s, exhibiting internationally and receiving numerous awards. Originally from Calazo (Bl), he welcomes his father who has come from the mountains to visit him. (*Credit: La Voce*)

The 1970s/151

***ALPINI*, LONDON, 1973**
Individually photographed at their annual dinner dance the *Alpini*, or Black Feathers (*Penne Nere*) as they are known, are one of the oldest associations in London, composed of men who have done their military service in the mountain regiments. Famous for their choir which practises every week and performs at events in the Italian Community, the *Alpini* form a key element of the London Italian Community. There is also a section in Wales, the *Alpini Sezione di Galles*. (*Credit: Studio Ernest*)

YOUNG WELSH ITALIANS ARE PRESENTED AT THE *QUIRINALE*, **ROME, 1975**
On a visit sponsored by the Italian Consulate in London, *Cavaliera* Maria Schiavo of Cardiff, second on the right, accompanies these second generation members and presents them to the President of the Italian Republic, *Presidente* Leone. Such a visit naturally provided these young people with a unique opportunity to learn more about their Italian heritage. The 'old' Italian Community of Wales had been supplemented by the post-Second World War influx of migrants, mainly from the south of Italy. *Cav.* Schiavo, herself from Sicily, continues today to be most active in the Welsh Italian Community and is an elected member of the Italian government-funded Committee of Italians Abroad (*Com.It.Es.*). (*Credit: M. Schiavo*)

COMMENDATORE GIUSEPPE GIACON IS PRESENTED TO PRESIDENT LEONE OF ITALY, ROME, 1975

A major international conference on emigration from Italy, the first of its kind, was held in Rome in 1975 with delegates from Italian Communities all over the world. *Comm.* Giacon was one of the representatives of Italians resident in Great Britain. This forum was invaluable to Community leaders who were able to present the particular problems facing their own Community and, at the same time learn about their international counterparts. Many links were forged at this conference, where one of the main topics of discussion was the issue of 'return migration' to Italy, something which was prevalent in the 1970s. The second conference of this nature was organised by the Italian government in 1988. (*Credit: ANSA*)

THE WEDDING OF MARIA GISO AND SALVATORE BOCCHINO, BEDFORD, 1973
Through the marriages of the second generation in Bedford, the all-important family ethos of the Community was maintained. Parents were hopeful that their off-spring might find a spouse from their own village of origin, but, where this was not possible due to a lack of potential partners, it was still important to marry a member of the Italian Community. Maria and Salvatore, pictured here, were in fact both born in Italy and were brought over to Bedford with their parents in the early 1950s. Both sets of parents came from villages in the province of Avellino. (*Credit: R. Giso*)

THE PROCESSION OF VILLAGE PATRON SAINTS, BEDFORD, 1975
After the Italian Church in Bedford was founded, it was important to the Community that each of its main *paesani* groups had statues of their village saints present in the church. A procession of these patron saints, similar to the processions in the south of Italy, has become a feature of Italian Community life in Bedford. The statues are carried out of the church, and in procession, are taken around the area which represents the old Italian quarter of the town. Here we see Santa Francesca, after whom the church is named, and who is always first in the procession. The other village saints are Sant'Angelo Muxaro (Ag) of the village of that name, San Lorenzo of Busso (Cb), San Ciriaco of Buonvicino (Cs), Santa Lucia of Cava Dei Tirreni (Sa), Sant'Antonio of Padova but who represents the migrants from Montefalcione (Av). San Guiseppe, the patron saint of workers, is also part of the procession. (*Credit: La Voce*)

PROCESSION OF THE *MADONNA DEL CARMINE*, LONDON, 1977
In our first close-up of the *Madonna*, we see that the statue is encircled with roses. There are six bearers this year, with four in fact carrying most of the weight. For the men of the Community it is an honour to take a turn in bearing the statue. Normally, the *Madonna* leaves from St Peter's Italian Church and the procession takes about forty minutes to complete its mile-long route around the old Italian quarter of Clerkenwell and back to the church. Italians continue to turn out in their thousands and line the route of the procession. (*Credit: B. Medici*)

CHAPTER NINE

The 1980s

The 1980s were an extremely interesting decade in the evolution of the British Italian Community and a number of changes occurred. Firstly, there was the immigration of a completely different type of Italian. With an expansion in the Italian diplomatic and official state presence in Britain, the number of highly educated Italians, particularly in London, expanded accordingly. In addition, with the internationalisation of banking and financial services, there was an influx of Italian bankers and brokers, again almost exclusively to London. Most of these people are posted here on a temporary basis, but they seek to enter and make an impact on British diplomatic, banking, cultural and social circles at a high level during their time here.

However, these high flyers are also part of the Italian Community, and are simply the latest group to have left Italy to come to this country to work. They add another layer to the rich mosaic of Italians in Britain, reflecting, in part, Italy's own prosperity and growing influence on world affairs. There is an overlap between this group and the more established Italian Communities, particularly for the government officials who are there to co-ordinate the provision of services to the Community, and who provide an official link with Italy. The Italian Community has always respected the Italian Ambassador to Britain and his Consuls; they receive invitations to all kinds of Community events.

Another major development in the 1980s was the increase in the number of associations formed within the Italian Community. From London outwards, a new wave of societies, circles and associations spread throughout the other 'old' Communities. Encouraged by the regional governments in Italy, these new associations are provincially and regionally based groups which bind together all migrants from the same province or region of origin. Thus, for example, the various associations of *Trentini, Campani* and *Liguri* were created, as well as many other new *Toscani* and *Emiliani* associations.

In the 'new' Communities, however, the growth in the number of associations was slower since such initiatives come from within the Community, and in the 'new' Communities there is not the same history of formal organisation. Here socialisation remains more informal, and club houses for all rather than specialist associations remain popular and well attended. One or two of the 'old' Italian Community clubs were still in existence, notably the *Mazzini Garibaldi Club* in London, over 120 years old, and also the *Casa d'Italia* in Glasgow, founded in 1935. However, the closure of the *Casa* in 1989 symbolised the reality that, in the 'old' Italian Communities, the need for a permanent, specifically Italian, club was no longer there. Another great loss to Italians was the closure of the Italian Hospital after almost a century of serving the Community.

Thirdly, throughout the 1980s, political activity in the Italian Community increased. This was partly due to the two European Parliamentary Elections of 1984 and 1989 which allowed Italians resident in Britain to vote for the Italian delegates at polling stations in this country. Naturally, this participation encouraged a knowledge of and involvement in Italian politics. In addition to this, there were the internal Community elections of 1986, the first of their kind, again organised on behalf of the Italian government by the Consulates. Part of a unique experiment in democracy at an international level, these elections enfranchised the entire Italian population to select their own leaders. Thus were born the four *Co.Em.It.* consultative committees, one for the London, Manchester, Edinburgh and Bedford areas, each with twelve members.

In the 1980s, the level of social and political activity in the Community began to approach a level which had not been attained since the 1930s.

MACARI'S, HERNE BAY, KENT COAST, 1985.
The Italian ice-cream industry in Britain was at its peak in the 1930s, particularly in coastal locations around the country. The scale and sumptuousness of some of the ice-cream parlours was impressive and there were several large family chains, notably the ones owned by the Forte and Notariani families. The Italian ice-cream trade has best survived in these coastal towns, often in the original premises. Macari's first opened in 1932 and was refitted in the 1950s, with a facade and interior which are still intact today. Elsewhere, inland, there are few Italian families left who make ice-cream in the traditional way, with fresh milk, on the premises. (*Credit: K. Sumner*)

NARDINI'S, LARGS, CLYDE COAST, 1985
Originally three brothers who came from Barga (Lu), Nardini is one of the oldest Italian family businesses in Scotland, having been established in 1890 in Paisley. Their ice-cream parlour and restaurant on the Clyde coast opened in the 1930s and is the last of the grand old cafés left in Scotland today, and continues to be popular with day trippers from Glasgow. The family business interests have now extended beyond the café and they also import refrigeration machinery from Italy for making ice-cream and for catering in general. (*Credit: A. Bavaro*)

RISTORANTE LA PARMIGIANA, GLASGOW, 1989
From left to right: Giovanni Sideri, the head waiter; Sandro Giovanazzi, the chef, who returned to Italy for his training; and his father, Angelo, the proprietor. As the name of the restaurant suggests, the Giovanazzi family originated in Parma, in Compiano (Pr) in fact, and are one of the very few families in Glasgow from this area of Italy. Giovanni Sideri is from Cagliari in Sardinia, also unusual for the Glasgow Italian Community; he, however, is a much more recent immigrant. The Giovanazzi family have a long history in catering, and La Parmigiana today is arguably the best proper Italian restaurant in Glasgow. (*Credit: A. Giovanazzi*)

CAVALIERE SERGIO COSTA, OF COSTA COFFEE, TALKING WITH THE QUEEN AT THE OPENING OF THE
NEW STATION AND HIS COFFEE BAR, READING 1989
Behind the bar, Marco Costa and Mireno Giacometti chat to the Duke of Edinburgh. Now to be found in several locations across the country, Costa brought the Italian-style coffee bar to this country. This exemplifies a new wave of Italian businesses in this country based on ideas successful in Italy today. Costa coffee is also now sold, vacuum packed, in supermarkets and is the first fresh good quality Italian coffee to be so widely available in this country.
(*Credit: S. Costa*)

FAZZI BROTHERS, GLASGOW, 1988

From left to right: Roberto Fazzi; Carlo Fazzi; Angelo Fazzi and Sandro Sarti. The maternal grandfather of Sandro Sarti, Peter Fazzi, emigrated from Vinchiana (Lu) in the 1890s and reached Scotland, as a second choice destination, around the turn of the century. He would have preferred to go to America and actually reached Ellis Island, but was refused entry on health grounds. By just after the First World War, he and two brothers had established themselves in a café business in Motherwell. Peter also travelled round the houses of Italian families selling them *spaghetti* and *pomodoro* and realised the need for a provisions store. The first Fazzi Bros. Italian grocery store was set up in 1935, growing from the door to door sales operation. The business has recently expanded to three stores, two of which also house Italian-style coffee bars. (*Credit: Glasgow Herald*)

GABRIELE AND VERONICA GRANDI, HOTELYMPIA EXHIBITION, LONDON, 1989

Now the major crockery and porcelain supplier to Italian catering establishments across the country, *La Porcellana* was founded in 1980 by Gabriele Grandi. Born in Ferravalle (Fe), he came to London in 1959 as a young man to join his father, one of the Italian prisoners of war who had decided to stay in this country after the war. Veronica Grandi is a third generation London Italian whose grandparents were from the province of Salerno and who had arrived in this country around the turn of the century. (*Credit; G. Grandi*)

ANITA RODDICK, NÉE PERELLA, OF THE BODY SHOP, 1985
From a small shop in Brighton which opened in 1976, selling only 25 natural products for skin and hair, Anita has built The Body Shop into an international chain of over a hundred shops. It now sells many different products based on natural ingredients from around the world. Anita's success is also due to the business sense initially fostered in the Littlehampton café, belonging to her Italian parents, where she grew up and worked at weekends and after school. (*Credit: La Voce*)

ANTONIO RIA, WORCESTER, 1987
The well known Italian photographer sifts through his photographs of the Worcester Italian Community, which he exhibited at the town's museum. Just visible on the right is one of Ceci, the Italian delicatessen shop in Worcester. The exhibition was organised and funded jointly by the Italian Consulate in Manchester and the *Co.Em.It.* (*Credit: Midland Newspapers*)

ELENA SALVONI (ON THE RIGHT) WITH MRS JOHN LOGIE BAIRD AT BIANCHI'S, LONDON, 1980S
Born in Clerkenwell Italian Colony, Elena Salvoni has spent a lifetime working in the prestigious Italian restaurants of Soho. She became the first female Italian *maître d'* at Bianchi's Restaurant, where she worked for thirty years. More recently she transferred to L'Escargot in Greek Street, and at 69 is now not only one of the very few female *maîtres d'*, but also one of the oldest in service. Through her many years of dedication, she has built up an impressive international network of famous friends who have enjoyed her hospitality. Here, she is pictured with the wife of John Logie Baird, the man who invented television. Logie Baird had conducted his experiments in the rooms which became Bianchi's restaurant. (*Credit: E. Salvoni*)

CAVALIERE **RANDO BERTOIA, WATCHMAKER, GLASGOW, 1989**
From Montereale Valcellina (Pn) in the region of Friuli, Rando initially came to Scotland as a boy
with his father in the 1920s. As a specialist *terrazzo* and mosaic worker, his father had been called
to work for Toffolo, a *paesano,* and the founder of the famous *terrazzo* firm in Glasgow. During
the Second World War, Rando survived the sinking of the *Arandora Star* and spent the remainder
of the war interned in Australia. On his return to Glasgow in 1945, he set up his watchmaking,
and now mainly watch repairing, business with his brother in Victoria Road. (*Credit: Glasgow
Herald*)

THE BRITISH ITALIAN LAW SOCIETY, LONDON, 1980

Formed by a group of British and Italian lawyers at the Middle Temple, the aim of the association is to foster closer ties between the Italian and British legal professions, and to promote greater understanding of the Italian legal system. A good number of the 150 members are British-born Italians who are able to use their knowledge of both languages and cultures to the full in their profession. Many are qualified in both Italian and British law. The Society has a very active programme of events and its level of co-ordination with Italian legal institutions is increasing as European integration gathers momentum. From left to right: *Avv*. Zani; *Avv*. Elia; *Avv*. Romito; *Avv*. Mills; Lord Salmon; *Avv*. Colombotti; *Avv*. Pini; *Avv*. Sammarco; *Avv*. Stabley; *Avv*. Davies. (*Credit: B. Medici*)

COCKTAIL PARTY, BANCO DI ROMA, LONDON, 1988

Pictured here are *Dott*. Marcello Tacci, *Dott*. Vittorio Sisto, director of *Banco di Roma* in London and Sir Jeremy Morse, Chairman of Lloyds Bank at a reception for the opening of the new premises of *Banco di Roma*, in Gresham Street in the City, attended by over 600 guests. The bank employs over 100 people and forms part of the growing international investment banking community in London specialising in money markets, foreign currency and financial futures trading in the new deregulated financial markets of both London and Italy. The large number of Italian managerial personnel at *Banco di Roma*, and the many other Italian banks in the City form part of a new stratum in the British Italian Community. (*Credit: La Voce*)

FESTA DELLA REPUBBLICA, EDINBURGH, 1983

The drinks party held on Italy's National Day is one of the main events of the British Italian Community's social calendar. 1983 was especially significant since, according to records held at the Italian Consulate General in Edinburgh, this was the centenary of the first documented permanent settlement of Italian immigrants in Scotland. More than a hundred Italians from all over Scotland attended this event. From left to right: *Signora* Nadia Dalziel; the Bishop of Aberdeen, Mario Conti; *Padre* Pietro Zorza, chaplain to the Italians in Scotland; *Signor* and *Signora* Tamburrino; *Signora* Lonardo, wife of the then Italian Consul General to Scotland. (*Credit: La Voce*)

THE ITALIAN CONSULATE GENERAL IS BLOWN UP, LONDON, 1980

The five-storey consular offices in Belgravia were wrecked by an explosion caused by an arson attack which ignited a gas main during the night of 23 March 1980. The building had been occupied by the Consulate since the 1950s, and the explosion destroyed documents on at least 140,000 Italians resident in the south of England. An Italian was found guilty at the Old Bailey for this attack, and also for a smaller fire at the Italian Education Offices near Victoria during the previous week. (*Credit: Press Association*)

AVV. OSVALDO FRANCHI, ON THE RIGHT, IS AWARDED THE *GRANDE UFFICIALE* BY THE ITALIAN GOVERNMENT, GLASGOW, 1988

The first Italian in Scotland to receive this prestigious honour, Osvaldo Franchi devoted his life to the promotion of the Italian language and culture, as well as being a tireless and creative worker within the Scottish Italian Community. As initiator, main contributor to, and president of, almost all the committees and bodies within the Scottish Italian Community, his sudden death in 1990 is an irreparable loss. From left to right: the Rev. James Clancy, Vicar General; the Consul General of Scotland, *Dott.* Rodolfo Buonavita; the Minister of the Italian Embassy, *Dott.* Muzi Falconi; the Lord Provost of Glasgow, Susan Baird and *Grande Ufficiale* Osvaldo Franchi. (*Credit: La Voce*)

A RELATIVE OF THE DECEASED CIRIACO FELICE AT HIS 'GARDEN GRAVE', BEDFORD, 1982

Such graves, common amongst the Italian Community, caused a controversy with Bedford Town Council in the early 1980s as the graves and plots interfered with cemetery maintenance policy. A similar row erupted in 1990 in Edinburgh where Italians have for several generations kept these sort of graves. As burial space became short in the Mount Vernon Cemetery in Edinburgh, digging began for fresh graves between the lines of burial plots, and some of the graves of Italians were damaged by tractors. The Cemetery claimed that family lairs exceeded the permitted size for burial plots. (*Credit: Bedfordshire County Press*)

THE KEEP FIT CLASS OF *CLUB DELLE DONNE*, LONDON, 1984

The Ladies Club, which was founded in 1984 by *Cavaliera* Roberta Mutti, sitting on the extreme right, presently has 230 members, and organises a number of initiatives involving both men and women in the London Italian Community. With the high levels of affluence and independence now prevalent within the Italian Community, the women, mainly married, have free time to organise activities with other Italian women, and this new association has proved extremely popular. Activities cover a range of events from flower arranging, talks, keep fit, and holidays abroad. The annual fashion show organised by the club is very successful and attracts sponsorship from some of the large Italian fashion houses. (*Credit: R. Mutti*)

THE YOUNG ITALIAN OLYMPICS, BARNET, 1980

First organised in 1980 by the Youth Club of St Peter's Italian Church, the *Olimpiadi della Giovantù Italiana* is now an outstanding feature of Italian Community life at a national level. The three day event, organised over the May bank holiday weekend, was an instant success in 1980, with over 500 participants. By 1990, this figure had risen to almost 1,000 young people. The teams are organised through the associations, clubs, and committees of the Community, which naturally allows for considerable adult participation too. The 1980 winners were the 'Italians Scotland' team with 15 gold, 13 silver and 12 bronze medals. Second were the *arrotini* and in fifth place came the Watford team. (*Credit: G. Alcorano*)

THE COMMITTEE OF THE NEWLY FORMED *ASSOCIAZIONE LIGURI NEL MONDO* **OUTSIDE THE TAVERNA ETRUSCA, LONDON, 1988**

Almost 100 *Liguri* gathered for a dinner to discuss preparations for 1992 which will be the 500th anniversary of the discovery of America by one of their own people, the *Genovese*, Cristoforo Colombo. The *Liguri* of London are composed mainly of the new wave of 1980s immigrants: the bankers, managers and government officials, but there are also people from the 'old' Italian Community, some of whom reached London through the Scottish, and particularly the Greenock, connection. (*Credit: L. Costello*)

ANNUAL DINNER DANCE OF THE *ASSOCIAZIONE LUCCHESI NEL MONDO*, **LONDON, 1980S**

One of the oldest regionally based associations in London, founded in 1970, the *Lucchesi nel Mondo* have around 230 members. There is also a section of *Lucchesi* based in Paisley, where many of the descendants of the original migrants from this area of Italy are located. When either one of these sections holds its annual dinner and dance, it is normal for members of the other to attend. Pictured here, speaking from the top table, is Mario Olla, who was the president of the region of Tuscany in the 1980s and was actively involved with many expatriate communities of *Toscani* throughout the world. It was an important occasion for the *Lucchesi* of London to host such a guest of honour at their dinner. (*Credit: B. Medici*)

The Whit Walk in Manchester continues, but has declined in popularity over the last ten years. The festival atmosphere is not, according to locals, quite as it used to be. The Italians, however, with the magnificent *Madonna*, a Calvary and a small statue carried by children of Sant'Antonio, which was introduced in the 1950s, have come increasingly to dominate the procession. Partly because of this, there has been pressure by the new Bishop of Salford either to limit or ban completely the Italian presence.
(*Credit: A. Rea*)

THE PROCESSION OF SAINTS, BEDFORD, 1983
Sant'Antonio is the patron of the migrants from Montefalcione (Av). Over 40 per cent of the migrants in Bedford are from the region of Campania and increasingly Sant'Antonio is becoming the main saint of the Community. Over half of all pilgrims who attend the procession follow this statue and many are very generous in their offerings. The gold chains attached to Sant'Antonio will go to the upkeep of the church and the cost of the *festa* which follows the procession.
(*Credit: A. Bavaro*)

EUROPEAN PARLIAMENTARY ELECTIONS, LONDON, 1984

Padre Gaetano Parolin points out that the polling station is Italian. The Italian population resident in Britain is entitled to vote for the Italian delegates to the European Community. The Italian consular authorities throughout the country were responsible for organising these elections in 1979, 1984 and 1989. In 1989 they organised almost a hundred polling stations up and down the country, strategically sited in or near the main Italian Communities. Apart from the European elections, the other main opportunity for the Italians in Britain to participate in politics is the internal Community elections, which also are organised by the Italian authorities (*Co.Em.It.*, 1986 and *Com.It.Es.*, 1991). (*Credit: La Voce*)

RADIO LONDRA, LONDON, 1986

The instigator and director, Wolfgang Bucci, explains operations to Laura Zanè. This Community radio station was launched in 1986 initially as a pirate station before gaining its wide range licence in 1989 against fierce competition. The station broadcasts every afternoon for two hours in Italian and a recent survey found that over 35 per cent of the London Italian Community listen in from time to time. The aim of *Radio Londra* is to keep the Italians up to date with news from Italy and, at the same time, to report on events within the local Italian Community. The recent introduction of live commentary coverage of Italian football on Sundays, for example, is very popular, but equally, interviews with the Ambassador and *personaggi* of the Italian Community are of great local interest. (*Credit: W. Bucci*)

MISS EMIGRANTE BECOMES *MISS ITALIA*, 1989

The beauty contests of the second generation became *Miss Italia* contests by the mid 1980s, reflecting the change in attitude towards emigration and the general strengthening of links between Italy and the expatriate Communities. Organised by the Association of Emigrant Families (ANFE) but also involving Italian politicians from Puglia, as well as musicians from Italy, this event was held in Bedford Town Hall and was attended by over 700 Italians from the south east of England. *Miss Italia* of Great Britain was 17 year old Ida Lucci of Slough. In second place was Luisa Biasi of Watford and third was Antonietta Spiniello of Bedford. (*Credit: La Voce*)

UNLOADING AND TESTING THE GRAPES, BEDFORD, 1985
Wine-making, in the traditional village way, using only grapes and barrel presses, is common in Italian Communities throughout Britain. In Bedford almost every family makes wine, usually between 500 and 1,000 litres, ensuring family and friends an annual supply of mainly red, fruity and natural wine. Sometimes cooperatives are formed and an individual is commissioned on behalf of a number of families, normally a group of *paesani*, to take a lorry over to Italy and transport back a consignment of grapes. Particular individuals within the Community are known to have great skill in wine-making and can often be called in if particular problems occur. Here, a van arrives outside one of the Italian shops in the heart of the Queen's Park Italian Community. The men test the grapes before carrying off their own allocation. (*Credit: A. Bavaro*)

FRANCESCO MARINARO ASSISTED BY HIS SON, SERGIO, MAKING WINE IN THEIR GARAGE, BEDFORD, 1985

Very few of the second generation make wine independently: the skill and expertise of the first generation *contadini* has not generally been absorbed by the more urbanised British-born. The same is true in other Italian Communities. Only the first generation of migrants, who have rural backgrounds, have the confidence to attempt wine-making in this country. It is doubtful if the current high levels of activity in wine-making, especially in the southern Italian Communities, will survive into the third generation. (*Credit: A. Bavaro*)

BOY WITH *PORCINI* MUSHROOMS, LONDON, 1985

The most famous area in Italy for mushrooms is the Val Taro (Pr). Some would say that the best mushrooms in the world grow there. Italians originating from here and other nearby wooded mountain areas of Italy and now resident in this country have brought their passion for mushrooms with them and one of the favourite pastimes, particularly of the London Italian Community, is to go hunting for *funghi*, or mushrooms, in woodlands around the capital. Locations of finds are closely guarded secrets. After a successful mushroom hunt, the crop is either frozen, dried, distributed to friends and relatives, or sold to grateful restaurateurs to satisfy the growing fashion for 'wild mushrooms' on the more sophisticated menus. (*Credit: A. Malvermi*)

A GAME OF CARDS, SUMMER 1983
Bedford or Busso? Peterborough or Petrella? Nottingham or Accettura? Such re-creation of southern Italian village environments in urban Britain is not uncommon, especially in the larger Italian Communities. *Paesani* like to come together in an informal manner, mainly in single sex groups, as they would do in their village in Italy. Although in Britain there is little opportunity for street life, loitering in the *piazza* or outside the bar, men are particularly adept at group activity which re-creates their village social patterns. It is popular to congregate at weekends, either in each others gardens during the summer months, or in the Italian provisions shops in winter. (*Credit: A. Bavaro*)

CELEBRATIONS AT BAR ITALIA, SOHO, WHEN ITALY WINS THE WORLD CUP, 1982
The jubilation at Italy's World Cup win in 1982 was uncontainable and it united almost the entire Italian Community in an unprecedented way. In cities and towns up and down the country there was an ethnic 'coming out of the closet' where Italians paraded and announced their win, up and down streets, in squares, in market places, all over the country. Nationalism and patriotism reached new heights. Old ladies dressed in black, normally reserved and indoors, joined the street celebrations. Ties with Italy were once again strongly reinforced. (*Credit: La Voce*)

WORLD CUP CELEBRATIONS, BEDFORD, 1982
Hundreds, perhaps thousands, of Italians, of all ages, appeared on the streets of Bedford the night Italy won the World Cup. They paraded around the town centre and congregated finally in Market Square, and, unable to conceal their general feeling of world wide triumph, scaled the monument of John Howard, the most revered of Bedford's citizens. The celebrations lasted well into the night for the jubilant members of the second generation, most of whom had been born in Bedford. (*Credit: Bedfordshire Times*)

CHAPTER TEN

The 1990s and Conclusion

As the new decade unfolds, the future of the Italian Community in Great Britain, which numbers at least 250,000 people, is bright. As Italy increasingly plays a role in Europe, so too will the British Italians identify with Europe and help Britain follow.

Today, as over 60 per cent of all Italians in Britain live in the south east, it is hard to resist the conclusion that London has become the dominant heartland of the Italian presence in this country. Not only has the immigration of the 1980s given a new layer to the Italian Community, adding a new and 'upper crust' to the overall structure, but the 'Europeanisation' of commerce, art and design and the professions, is also centred on London. Furthermore, new institutions like the *Accademia Italiana* in Knightsbridge, remind us of the wealth of Italy's artistic heritage. The continuing business success of Lord Forte and his family, the awakening interest of the Press in all forms of European cultural life already active in London, and, of course, the ever-evolving catering connection, all make it very exciting to be part of the London-based British Italian Community in the early 1990s.

However, London does not have it all its own way, and both 'old' and 'new' Communities remain alive and vigorous. This is perhaps especially true of the large southern Italian post-World War Two Communities which in the second generation have experienced very little assimilation. These groups are presently clinging to their traditions, and thanks to a considerable amount of contact with Italy, perhaps they will now be able — more than at any time in the past — to grow and change in an Italian way as Italy itself develops. Large numbers of these migrants maintain two homes, one here and one in Italy, although not always in their village of origin, and as this Community has reached retirement age, the old fashioned notion of 'going back', as a permanent step, is no longer so appropriate.

In many of the 'old' Communities too, a great deal of Italian activity and way of life remains. For example, President Cossiga of Italy made an impromptu visit to the dinner dance of the *Associazione Parmigiani* in Scotland after completing his popular state visit to this country in November 1990. The National Library of Scotland in 1991 hosted a major 'Italian Scots' exhibition. Fiat have funded a new chair of Italian language and literature at Oxford University, the Fiat Serena Chair. In Scotland and Manchester, for example, there are individuals who are the fourth and fifth generation of the original immigrants, but whose blood is 100 per cent Italian. Inevitably these people, who often speak only a little Italian, consider themselves to be Italian.

In addition, many very old family businesses are still in operation, gaining a new injection of skill, expertise and creativity from the third and fourth generation who have been educated to the highest levels both in this country and in Italy, and many of whom are Britain's first truly European citizens. Many other descendants of the 'old' Communities now participate at the highest levels in the social, economic and political life of their local towns and cities and several of them including Hugh Rossi, Michael Portillo, and recently David Bellotti have entered Parliament. There are a large number of Italians prominent in the Arts (Lord Palumbo, Sir Eduardo Paolozzi, Richard De Marco, Tom Conti, to name but a few). Italians now make contributions at every level of British society.

The study of the history of the British Italian Community teaches us of its proud heritage and reminds us of the major contribution to the life of Britain over the past century and a half made by the Italian immigrants and their descendants. That passage of time has witnessed setbacks and surprises, but these have been overcome with hard work and perseverance. Now, on the brink of a new golden era for the Italians in Britain, we can surely all unite in saying 'Italians Forward'.

RENZA DONATI, DINGWALL, 1990
From Castelnuovo Garfagnana (Lu), the Donati family arrived in Dingwall in the north of Scotland in the 1940s having spent many years in Glasgow. An uncle in Inverness effected the transfer, finding the shop in Dingwall for them. Now they are one of two Italian families in the town, the Onesti family from Barga (Lu) being the other. The Donati family are in the ice-cream business and the Onesti family in fish and chips. The two shops are opposite each other in Main Street. Despite geographical distance and isolation, Renza Donati's cheerful and hard-working disposition typifies the spirit upon which so much of the British Italian Community has been built over the last 150 years. (*Credit: T. Colpi*)

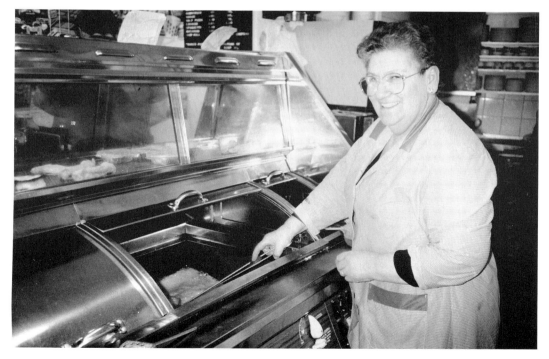

MARIA MANCINI, FRYING FISH, ROYAL CAFÉ, AYR, 1990
Arriving in this Ayrshire seaside town from Atina (Fr) after her marriage to Michael Mancini in 1946, Maria became a member of one of the oldest Italian family businesses in Ayr. She has worked here ever since, raising her family at the same time, displaying the strength typical of the Scottish Italian woman in remaining central to both her family and her business. (*Credit: T.Colpi*)

CAVALIERE RICHARD DE MARCO, OBE, RSW
A well known gallery director in Edinburgh and a leading thinker and innovator in the international art world, Richard De Marco is enormously proud of, and interested in, his Italian heritage. Indeed, one of his lifelong missions has been to bring the beauty and the passion of Italian and other European art and culture to the people of Edinburgh. (*Credit: R. De Marco*)

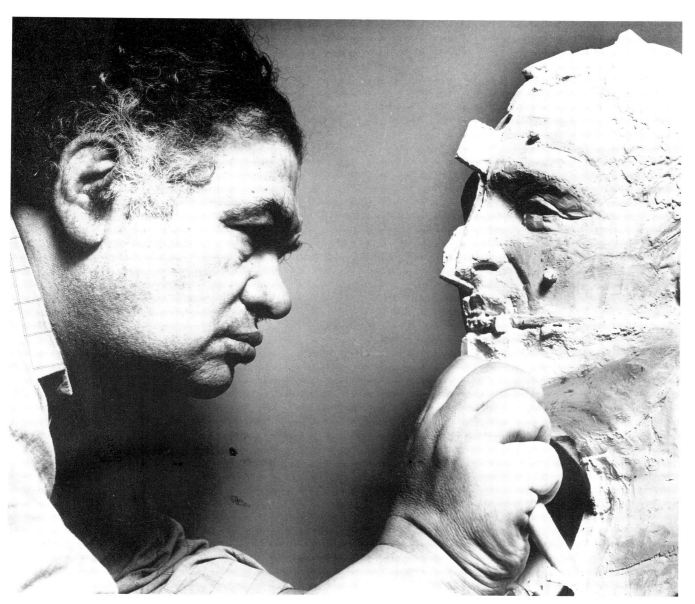

SIR EDUARDO PAOLOZZI, CBE, RA
Sculptor of international repute, Sir Eduardo works here on plaster for a portrait bust of the architect Richard Rogers. The bronze sculpture of this work is now in the National Portrait Gallery, London. Originally from an Edinburgh Italian family, Sir Eduardo lost his father on the *Arandora Star*, and perhaps partly because of this, his work continues to be influenced by his own *italianatà*. (*Credit: E. Paolozzi*)

PAUL COLETTI, VIOLIST
Born in Edinburgh of parents from the Frosinone area of Italy, and a former pupil of Yehudi
Menuhin, Paul Coletti is now Professor of Music at Baltimore's Peabody Conservatory and is a
violist of growing international reputation. (*Credit: L. Coletti*)

FRANCIS ROSSI, GUITARIST
A third generation London Italian, Francis Rossi
has achieved worldwide recognition and endur-
ing popularity with his band, Status Quo.
(*Credit: S. Porter*)

UMBERTO DI ZENZO, LONDON, 1990
Here the artist explains a cube of light at his 'Art Light' exhibition held at the Italian Institute of Culture, London. The exhibition was facilitated by sponsorship from the *Comune* of Serino (Av), where Di Zenzo was born. (*Credit: U. Di Zenzo*)

FOUNDER OF THE *ACCADEMIA ITALIANA*, ROSA MARIA LETTS, AT THE OPENING CEREMONY WITH THE ITALIAN AMBASSADOR, H. E. BORIS BIANCHERI, LONDON, 1989
This major initiative in promoting Italian art and culture in this country was funded by the sponsorship of 25 Italian firms and many other sources. It now forms one of the major venues for the Arts in Great Britain. (*Credit: La Voce*)

THE 50TH ANNIVERSARY OF THE SINKING OF THE *ARANDORA STAR*, LONDON, 1 JULY 1990
Of the original 266 survivors of the *Arandora Star*, only 21 are still alive at the time of writing. Here, at a ceremony at the Italian Church, the able bodied were awarded, in person, the prestigious title of *Cavaliere al Merito della Repubblica Italiana* by the Italian government. Several from Scotland and Wales were unable to travel to attend the ceremony. Standing from left to right: *Cav.* Giorgio Scola; *Cav.* Riccardo Lombardelli; *Cav.* Gino Guarnieri; *Cav.* Rando Bertoia; *Cav.* Luigi Beschizza. Kneeling, *Cav.* Nicola Cua and, seated, *Cav.* Pietro Beschizza. (*Credit: T. Colpi*)

PRESIDENT COSSIGA OF ITALY AT THE NATIONAL LIBRARY OF SCOTLAND, EDINBURGH, 1990
After his 1990 state visit to Britain, President Cossiga met with the Italian Communities at gatherings in both London and Glasgow. Here at the National Library for Scotland in Edinburgh, he heard of plans for the June to November 1991 Italian Scots Exhibition. Shaking hands with President Cossiga, who is on the left, in front of the Consul General to Scotland, *Dott.* Rodolfo Buonavita, is Michael Strachan, Chairman of the Board of Trustees of the Library. (*Credit: C. Giglio*)

THE PROCESSION OF THE *MADONNA DEL CARMINE*, LONDON, 1990

In recent years, the statue of the *Madonna*, which had been made in Italy in the early 1880s, had been deteriorating and there was concern in the Community about its preservation. The old *figurinai* were called to the rescue and men who had worked in the statuette industry in the 1950s were asked to make an exact replica. The new *Madonna*, shown here, is hollow and therefore lighter to transport during the procession. The original statue now remains permanently inside the church. (*Credit: T. Colpi*)

THE *FESTA* AT WARNER STREET, AFTER THE PROCESSION, LONDON, 1990

On a golden summer's day, London's Italians turned out in their thousands for the annual street party in the traditional Italian style, in the old Colony. Many of the associations had a stall, either selling food and drinks associated with their own part of Italy, such as the *Veneti* and their *salsicci*, or offering some entertainment such as the *Alpini* with their coconut shy. Festivities carried on late into the evening. (*Credit: T. Colpi*)

APPENDIX ONE

GLOSSARY OF ITALIAN WORDS AND TERMS

ACCADEMIA	Academy
ALPINI	Mountain soldiers of the Italian army
AMICI	Friends
AMICI VAL CENO GALLES	Friends of the Val Ceno in Wales
A.N.F.E.	*Associazione Nazionale Famiglie Emigrati*
ARDITTO/ARDITTI	First assault soldier/special crack units
ARROTINO/ARROTINI	Knife grinder/s. These emigrants came from the Val Rendena now in the province of Trento
ASSISTENZA	Help, assistance
ASSOCIAZIONE	Association
AVVOCATO (Avv.)	Lawyer
BALDACCHINO	Canopy
BARGHIGIANI	People from the small town of Barga (Lu)
BELLA FIGURA	Favourable impression
BEFANA	Epiphany. Good Witch
BERSAGLIERI	Regiment of the Italian Army
BOMBONIERE	Keepsakes. For both christenings and weddings, *bomboniere* are distributed to all the guests as a keepsake of the event. Some sugared almonds are the basis of the gift, but these are attached to gifts of varying value from small trinkets to solid silver bells.
CACCIATORI	Hunters
CALABRESI	People from the region of Calabria
CAMPANI	People from the region of Campania
CASA	House. *Casa d'Italia* – House of Italy
CAVALIERE (Cav.)	Title of civil merit. Knight
CIOCIARIA	Geographical area name relating roughly to the province of Frosinone, but in the past also including sections of the provinces of Isernia and Caserta: the river Liri Valley area. People from this area were often, mistakenly, called *Napoletani*
CIOCIARI	People from the *Ciociaria*
CLUB DELLE DONNE	Ladies Club
CO.AS.IT.	*Comitato di Assistenza Scuole Italiane*
CO.EM.IT.	*Comitati Emigrazione Italiana*. Italian Emigration Committee (1986)
COMBATTENTI	Soldiers
COM.IT.ES.	*Comitati Italiani all'Estero*. Italian Committees Abroad (1991)
COMMENDATORE (Comm.)	Title of civic merit – superior to *Cavaliere*
COMPARI	Godparents, for a christening. Best man and woman for a wedding
COMUNE	Smallest administrative division in Italy. The *comune* comes after the region and the province in Italy's three-tier administrative system
CONDIZIONE	Condition
CONTADINO/CONTADINI	Peasant, farmer/s
COPPA CONSOLE GENERALE	The Consul General Cup
CROCE DI GUERRA	War Cross/decoration
DONNA/DONNE	Woman/Ladies

DOPOSCUOLA	After school
DOTTORE (Dott.)	Title given to person with a university degree
ECCO UN POCO	Here is a little
EMIGRANTE	Emigrant
EMILIANI	People from the region of Emilia
EX COMBATTENTI	Veteran soldiers
FASCIO/FASCI	Fascist club/s
FASCISTI	Members of the Fascist movement
F.A.S.F.A.	*Federazione delle Associazioni e Comitati Scuola Famiglia*
FESTA	Holiday, Saint's Day, Festival, Party
FESTA DEI NONNI	Grandparents' Day
FESTA DELLA REPUBBLICA	Festival of Italy's National Day
FIGURINAIO/FIGURINAI	Makers and travelling sellers of statuettes and figurines
F.I.L.E.F.	*Federazione Italiana Lavoratori Emigrati e Famiglie*
FRIULANI	People from the region of Friuli
FUNGHI	Mushrooms
GARFAGNANA	Geographical area relating to the northern half of the province of Lucca, in the Upper Valley of the River Serchio
GARIBALDINI	Followers of Garibaldi. *Ex Garibaldini* – former followers of Garibaldi
GARZONE/GARZONI	Boy Apprentice/s
GENOVESE	Person from Genova. Genova is in the region of Liguria
GIORNATA DELLE FEDI	Day of the Wedding Rings
GIOVENTÙ, GIOVINEZZA	Youth, young people
GRANDE UFFICIALE (Gran.Uff.)	Highest title of civil merit
LIGURI	People from the region of Liguria
LIGURI NEL MONDO	*Liguri* of the world
LUCCHESI	People from the province of Lucca
LUCCHESI NEL MONDO	*Lucchessi* of the world
LONDRA	London
MADONNA	Our Lady
MADONNA DEL CARMINE	Our Lady of Mount Carmel
MADONNA DEL ROSARIO	Our Lady of the Rosary
MOLETA	Wheel barrow equipment of the *arrotini*
MONDO	World
MOR(R)A	Guessing game
NAPOLETANI	People from the Naples area
OLIMPIADI	Olympics
OLIMPIADI DELLA GIOVANTÙ	Young Olympics
O MELTIS	The Meltis (factory in Bedford)
PADRE	Father, Priest
PADRONE/PADRONI	*Padrone* translates literally as master. The root word is *padre*, father. In the migratory context the translation would be either master, boss or patron
PAESE	Village/place
PAESANO/PAESANI	Fellow villager/person from the same village
PARMIGIANI	People from the province of Parma
PASSEGGIATA	Walk, promenade
PENNE NERE	Black feathers or *Alpini*
PERSONAGGI	Personalities, VIPs
PIAZZA	Square
POMODORO	Tomato/tomato puree for pasta sauce
PORCINI	A type of edible mushroom

PRIMA COMUNIONE	First Communion
PROSCIUTTO	Ham
QUIRINALE	Italian Parliament
RADIO LONDRA	Radio London
RISTORANTE	Restaurant
SACRIFICI	Sacrifices
SALSICCI	Spicy home-made sausages
SAN/SANTA	Saint
SCAMPAGNATA	Picnic. Countryside excursion
SIESTA	Afternoon nap
SIGNOR/SIGNORA	Mr/Mrs
SIGNORINA/SIGNORINE	Miss. Unmarried girls/women
TERAZZO	Specialist floor work
TOSCANI	People from the region of Tuscany
TRATTORIA/E	Informal restaurant/s
TRENTINI	People from the province of Trento
VENETI	People from the region of Veneto
VIAGGIATORI	Travellers
VOCE	Voice
LA VOCE DEGLI ITALIANI IN GRAN BRETAGNA	The voice of the Italians in Great Britain
ZAMPOGNE	Bagpipes from the *Ciociaria*

APPENDIX TWO

LIST OF ITALIAN PROVINCIAL ABBREVIATIONS

(Ag)	Agrigento	Sicilia	(Me)	Messina	Sicilia
(Al)	Alessandria	Piemonte	(Mi)	Milano	Lombardia
(An)	Ancona	Marche	(Mo)	Modena	Emilia Romagna
(Ao)	Aosta	Valle d'Aosta	(Na)	Napoli	Campania
(Ar)	Arezzo	Toscana	(No)	Novara	Piemonte
(Ap)	Ascoli Piceno	Marche	(Nu)	Nuoro	Sardegna
(At)	Asti	Piemonte	(Or)	Oristano	Sardegna
(Av)	Avellino	Campania	(Pd)	Padova	Veneto
(Ba)	Bari	Puglia	(Pa)	Palermo	Sicilia
(Bl)	Belluno	Veneto	(Pr)	Parma	Emilia Romagna
(Bn)	Benevento	Campania	(Pv)	Pavia	Lombardia
(Bg)	Bergamo	Lombardia	(Pg)	Perugia	Umbria
(Bo)	Bologna	Emilia Romagna	(Ps)	Pesaro	Marche
(Bz)	Bolzano	Trentino Alto Adige	(Pe)	Pescara	Abruzzo
(Bg)	Brescia	Lombardia	(Pc)	Piacenza	Emilia Romagna
(Br)	Brindisi	Puglia	(Pi)	Pisa	Toscana
(Ca)	Cagliari	Sardegna	(Pt)	Pistoia	Toscana
(Cl)	Caltanissetta	Sicilia	(Pn)	Pordenone	Friuli Venezia Giulia
(Cb)	Campobasso	Molise	(Pz)	Potenza	Basilicata
(Ce)	Caserta	Campania	(Rg)	Ragusa	Sicilia
(Ct)	Catania	Sicilia	(Ra)	Ravenna	Emilia Romagna
(Cz)	Catanzaro	Calabria	(Rc)	Reggio Calabria	Calabria
(Ch)	Chieti	Abruzzo	(Re)	Reggio Emilia	Emilia Romagna
(Co)	Como	Lombardia	(Ri)	Rieti	Lazio
(Cs)	Cosenza	Calabria	(Roma)	Roma	Lazio
(Cr)	Cremona	Lombardia	(Ro)	Rovigo	Veneto
(Cn)	Cuneo	Piemonte	(Sa)	Salerno	Campania
(En)	Enna	Sicilia	(Ss)	Sassari	Sardegna
(Fe)	Ferrara	Emilia Romagna	(Sv)	Savona	Liguria
(Fi)	Firenze	Toscana	(Si)	Siena	Toscana
(Fg)	Foggia	Puglia	(Sr)	Siracusa	Sicilia
(Fo)	Forlì	Emilia Romagna	(So)	Sondrio	Lombardia
(Fr)	Frosinone	Lazio	(Ta)	Taranto	Puglia
(Ge)	Genova	Liguria	(Te)	Teramo	Abruzzo
(Go)	Gorizia	Friuli Venezia Giulia	(Tr)	Terni	Umbria
(Gr)	Grosseto	Toscana	(To)	Torino	Piemonte
(Im)	Imperia	Liguria	(Tp)	Trapani	Sicilia
(Is)	Isernia	Molise	(Tn)	Trento	Trentino Alto Adige
(Aq)	L'Aquila	Abruzzo	(Tv)	Treviso	Veneto
(Sp)	La Spezia	Liguria	(Ts)	Trieste	Friuli Venezia Giulia
(Lt)	Latina	Lazio	(Ud)	Udine	Friuli Venezia Giulia
(Le)	Lecce	Puglia	(Va)	Varese	Lombardia
(Li)	Livorno	Toscana	(Ve)	Venezia	Veneto
(Lu)	Lucca	Toscana	(Vc)	Vercelli	Piemonte
(Mc)	Macerata	Marche	(Vr)	Verona	Veneto
(Mn)	Mantova	Lombardia	(Vi)	Vicenza	Veneto
(Ms)	Massa-Carrara	Toscana	(Vt)	Viterbo	Lazio
(Mt)	Matera	Basilicata			

ITALY: AREAS AND REGIONS

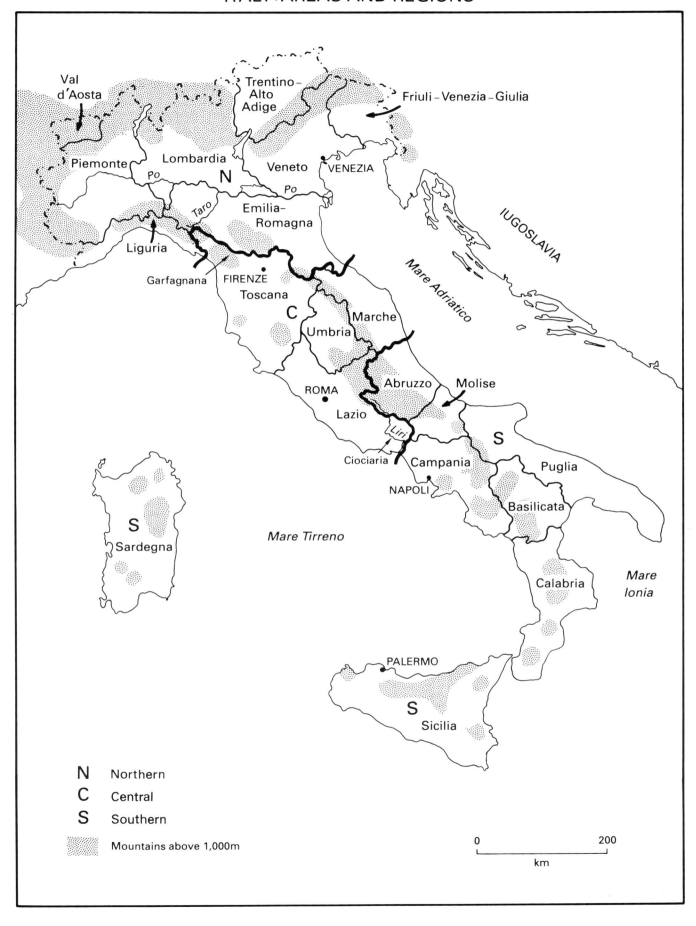

Val
d'Aosta

Trentino–
Alto
Adige

Friuli – Venezia – Giulia

Piemonte

Lombardia

Veneto

VENEZIA

N

Po

Po

Taro

Emilia–
Romagna

IUGOSLAVIA

Liguria

Garfagnana

FIRENZE

Toscana

Mare Adriatico

C

Marche

Umbria

Abruzzo

Molise

ROMA

Lazio

Liri

S

Ciociaria

Campania

Puglia

NAPOLI

Basilicata

S

Sardegna

Mare Tirreno

Calabria

Mare
Ionia

PALERMO

S

Sicilia

N   Northern

C   Central

S   Southern

Mountains above 1,000m

0   200

km